British Trams
in Camera

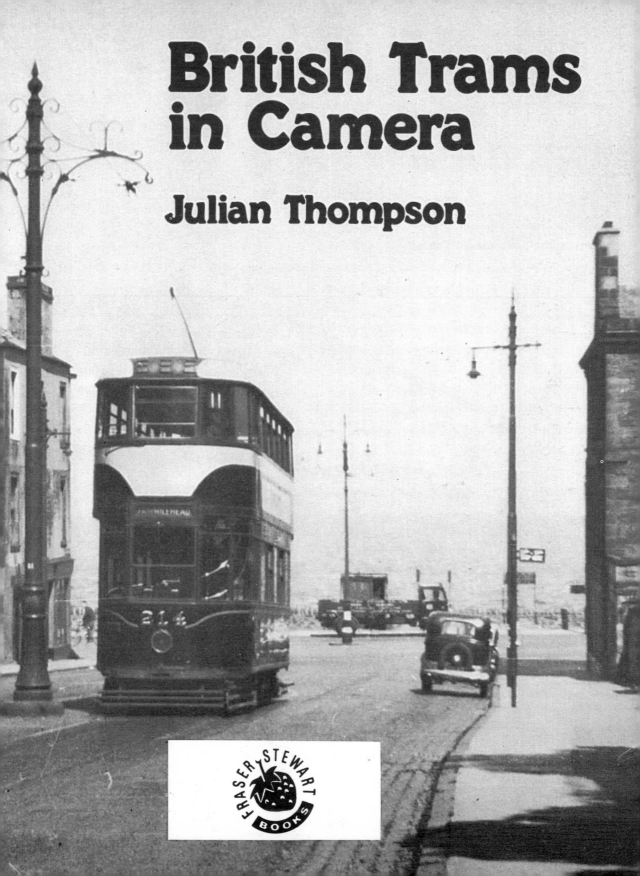

British Trams
in Camera

Julian Thompson

TRAMS IN CAMERA

First published 1978

ISBN 1 874723 23 0

All rights reserved. No part of this book may be
reproduced or transmitted in any form or by any
means, electronic or mechanical, including photo-
copying, recording or by any information storage
and retrieval system, without permission from the
Publisher in writing.

© Ian Allan Ltd 1978

This edition published 1992 by Fraser Stewart Book
Wholesale Ltd, Abbey Chambers, 4 Highbridge Street,
Waltham Abbey, Essex EN9 1DQ, produced by
The Promotional Reprint Company Ltd, UK.

Printed in Czechoslovakia
50591

Contents

Foreword   7
Glossary   8
London   10
The Swansea & Mumbles Railway   28
Birmingham   30
Leicester   36
Llandudno & Colwyn Bay Electric Railway   40
Howth   46
Liverpool   48
Stockport   52
Sheffield   56
Grimsby & Immingham Electric Railway   66
Leeds   68
Blackburn   80
Blackpool   82
Manx Electric Railway   90
Belfast   96
Glasgow   100
Dundee   108
Edinburgh   112
Tickets   126

Foreword

First of all I wish to express my sincere thanks to Anne Ford-Lloyd, FRPS, for her excellent and painstaking work in making enlargements from negatives taken by Gerald Druce and myself. These previously unpublished photographs show the tramcar in its natural workaday surroundings, which the artificial atmosphere of a museum cannot hope to capture. I am greatly indebted to Gerald Druce for reading and correcting the manuscript, which he encouraged me to prepare in the first place, and for supplying much invaluable information.

This book aims to present a broad cross-section of electric tramway undertakings which survived World War II; in its preparation I have been helped by certain publications, and wish to thank the authors of and contributors to the following:

Balham, Tooting & Streatham News & Mercury
Birmingham Transport ABC W. A. Camwell
Buses Illustrated
Edinburgh's Transport, D. L. G. Hunter
Evening News, London
Evening Standard, London
Great British Tramway Networks, W. H. Bett and J. C. Gillham
Modern Tramway
Modern Transport
South London Observer
South London Press
Star, London
The Story of Leicester's Trams, K. W. Smith.

Though it is easy to be wise after the event, I have made no attempt to explain the failure of tramways in Britain. Few undertakings had even a reasonable proportion of modern cars, while even fewer were prepared to consider development of their systems as rapid transit; most were content to cling to obsolete and worn-out equipment at any price, presenting the choice as that between ancient trams and modern buses! It is tragic that the activities of the growing body of tramway enthusiasts in Britain have perforce largely degenerated into a veneration and hunt for relics.

Even quite small Continental tramways have been thoroughly modernised in all respects. In Britain the re-introduction of tramways is being seriously considered, while construction of a light rapid transit line at Newcastle has already started. Readers may be interested to learn that the story of tramways in the German city of Freiburg plays an important part in a study of transport in the area, which I am now preparing.

Julian Thompson

Left: Freiburg im Breisgau: View looking west across the older part of the city, with a GT 4 articulated car passing through the Schwabentor. (13.5.72)

Glossary

Air-Wheel/Air-Track Brake non-automatic brake actuated by compressed air in a cylinder, and acting on wheels via brake blocks, or on rails via brake shoes.

Automatic Points points worked by electric contact on conductor wire, power being applied by driver to alter points only.

Body-Working flexing of car body, most pronounced on lower deck, caused by strains of starting and stopping.

Bogie one of two swivelling four-wheel trucks on which car body is mounted.

Bulkhead internal reinforcement of car body, between balcony (on upper deck) and platform (on lower deck) and saloons.

Centre-Pole Construction poles between tracks, from which overhead is suspended by bracket arms.

Change-Pit changeover point between conduit and overhead systems of current collection, for inserting or removing plough.

Changeover Switch driver's switch for altering electrical connections for current collectors at change-pit

Check Rail rail inserted inside running rail to limit lateral movement of wheels.

Composite Construction wooden framework with metal panelling.

Conduit Point Tongue tongue in conduit slot, connected to track point tongues, ensuring correct path of current collector.

Conduit System of Current Collection positive and negative rails in tube beneath road, usually with centre slot through which collector passes.

Controller speed control of tramcar, actuated by handle, in normal practice moved clockwise for acceleration, anti-clockwise for braking.

Corrugated Track irregularities on rail surface at right angles to direction of travel, conducive of noise and vibration.

Dash platform panel of car, also known as 'apron'.

Dead Section (of Conduit) interruption of current rails at points, crossings and end of electrical sections.

Extra Car additional car run to strengthen normal service.

Flat Wheel part of wheel tyre worn flat by skidding, recognisable in service by regular banging sound.

Flush Panel flat lower deck side of car, as opposed to traditional two-panel construction.

Inside-Frame Bogie axles mounted inside wheels, instead of normal arrangement with end of axles and outside frames.

Interlaced Track device for saving space on double track, whereby the right-hand rail of each track is laid between rails of adjacent track.

Loading Island refuge for passengers, situated alongside track.

Loop short section of double track on otherwise single line, where cars can pass.

Magnetic Track Brake braking by means of electro-magnetic attraction between brake shoes and rails.

Maximum Traction Truck truck with large driving wheels and small idling wheels; the driving wheels bear some 65% of the car weight, and are usually at the ends of the car.

Narrow Gauge gauge narrower than standard gauge; normally refers to 4ft or 3ft 6in gauge.

Notch power or braking position on tramcar controller.

Open Balcony open end to top deck.

Operating Costs Per Car Mile average of all expenses incurred per car mile run in service.

Pitching fore and aft movement of car, caused by loose rail joints.

Plough current collector on conduit system of current collection, inserted or removed at change pit.

Private Right of Way reserved track remote from public roads.

Radial Truck four-wheel truck, each axle of which can pivot on curves.

Reserved Track strip reserved for tramcars alongside roads or in centre of dual carriageway.

Resilient Wheel wheel with rubber insert between steel tyre and wheel centre.

Rheostatic Brake use of car motors as dynamos for braking down to very low speed, after which the hand brake was used for the final stop and holding the car.

Road depot track in particular; in tramway parlance often synonym for 'track'.

Rocker Panel lower panel of lower deck side (often concave).

Sanding deposit of sand dropped from pipes before driving wheels to prevent wheel slip.

Span Wire wire spanning roadway to carry conductor wire.

Special Car unscheduled car for special event.

Standard Car design of car built in quantity by an undertaking; does not refer to any particular type, for there was no British Standard Car.

Standard Gauge 4ft 8½in.

Swaying side to side movement of car, result of irregular rail levels.

Toastrack Car open single deck car with cross benches.

Transfer Ticket ticket allowing change of cars to complete journey.

Traverser moveable platform with short length of track, running at right angles to and alignable with depot tracks.

Trolley Reverser overhead arranged to form a reversing triangle, which trolley pole automatically follows.

Truck four-wheel carriage on which body is mounted.

Turning circle curved loop line for reversing car.

Vestibule closed and windscreened ends to lower deck platform.

Waist Panel side panel below lower deck windows (often convex).

Workman Ticket cheap early morning ticket, usually issued up to 8am.

Works Car non-passenger carrying car, for permanent way, stores or shunting duties.

The car involved in the Lavender Hill accident of August 23, 1950 is seen in the right background of this view at Penhall Road; in the foreground are works cars 05 (left) and 034. (27.9.50)

London

In the last few years of tramway operation, much money and effort were expended in making improvements and renewals which were to be very short-lived. London Transport embarked on an extensive overhaul programme, which included many of the older cars. It is true that a close examination of the paintwork often revealed a new coat on top of the old. In an attempt to stiffen the wooden bodywork, a number of the ex-LCC E/1 cars, together with some of the similar ex-Croydon and ex-Walthamstow cars, were strengthened with external bracing from early 1949 onwards: the last standard E/1s were withdrawn only three years later. The insinuation that the cars were still fitted with wartime blackout masks on headlamps was dispelled when London Transport insisted that the mask was a special post-war type: it provided a driving light superior to that used prior to 1939, and had been evolved to meet legal requirements regarding anti-dazzle and the showing of a rear light.

Delays in service, mainly due to the breakdown of cars or of the conduit current collection system, occurred frequently in the last years, but were probably not numerous in relation to the size of the network. The daily traveller most likely learnt from his paper that there had been another 'tram hold-up' as it was termed; even when cars became stranded for a few minutes on a 'dead' section of the conduit, where one track crossed or joined another, it was dutifully reported by the hostile evening papers.

There were often delays when changing crews at Camberwell, New Cross and Telford Avenue Depots. Referring to this in a letter to the *South London Press* of January 14, 1949, a Mr A. E. Southernwood made the sensible suggestion that bus and tram workers should receive a bonus every three months if they showed a punctual record. 'One often sees half a dozen trams held up at Camberwell Green because the

Below: Newly-overhauled ex-West Ham Corporation car 337 in Blackfriars Road. (2.4.51)

Top right: E/1 car 1802, with body strengthened with external bracing, in South Lambeth Road at Stockwell Station. (Spring 1949)

Bottom right: A disabled E/1 car on the siding in Blackfriars Road at Stamford Street. A conduit hatch is lying on the road beside the car. (1949)

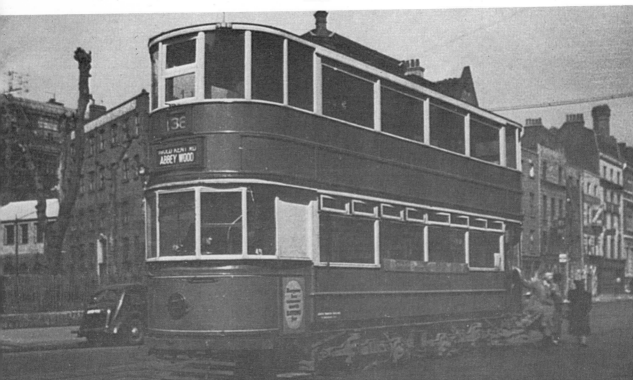

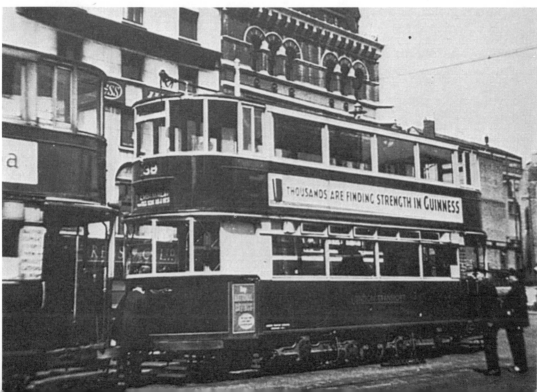

front car is waiting for a new crew. If the crew doesn't arrive, the passengers are turned out and the car taken out of service, and that means a gap of 15 (!) minutes between two cars on that service.' There was much complaint about inadequate tram services in Bermondsey on routes 68 and 70 in the 1948-50 period. In early 1950 London Transport regretted that the routes could not be strengthened, since there was no further stock to draw upon; the bunching of trams on Old Kent Road was admitted, but was blamed on congestion at the Elephant.

Many people do not realise, and few could, that the removal of street tramways in Britain was Government policy. Generally the replacement of tramways by other forms of transport was justified to the public on economic and traffic grounds. However in November 1949 the Ministry of Transport showed its true colours by stating that fixed tracks were to be replaced as soon as, and whenever possible; whether trolleybuses or motor buses took the place of trams was a local concern.

After the scheme for the conversion of the tramways had been announced on March 4, 1949, things moved quickly, and work on Wandsworth and Clapham Depots was proceeding by November. Wandsworth Depot was converted to overhead working, cars changing over to overhead in the Jews Row approach to the depot. By mid-summer 1950 the rear part of Clapham Depot had been demolished. The future scrap yard at Penhall Road near Woolwich was virtually complete early in 1950. Construction of new bus garages at Stockwell and Peckham, which were important to the tramway conversion, providing room for 200 and 125 vehicles respectively, started early in 1950; work at Stockwell was delayed by difficulties in land acquisition.

By February 26, 1950 Thornton Heath Depot and

TRAMS DIVERTED AFTER HOLD-UP

Tramcars on routes 10, 16, 18 and 33 had to be diverted via Stockwell Road and Clapham Road to-day after tramcar on up-track in Brixton Road had developed defect.

Passengers were delayed five minutes. One tramcar was held up for 21 minutes.

Top: Turnout under construction in Lambeth Palace Road at County Hall, showing (in foreground) hatch covers at branching of conduit slot. (24.7.50)

Above: An admirably detailed report of a minor tramway breakdown, from the *Evening Standard* of 5.11.48.

Left: The scene at the west side of Wandsworth Depot during conversion to bus operation. The conduit has been altered to run clear of the track (right foreground). (16.7.50)

Top right: E/1 car 1656 in partially dismantled state at Penhall Road scrap yard: this car was burnt on October 2 1950. (6.9.50)

Right: Maguire pattern maximum traction truck at Penhall Road. (27.9.50)

canteen, vacated in favour of Purley Depot, had been completely demolished to make way for a bus garage; by April the site had been cleared. The roof of the smaller south shed at Telford Avenue, where work had started at the end of December 1949, had been dismantled by the end of April 1950: until February at least 12 cars were still parked there without current. There was a right of way between the Telford Avenue sheds for a Metropolitan Water Board main to an adjoining reservoir. Of the original building, only the wing walls remained, and a special difficulty was altering the floor to provide a level site for 125 buses in place of 90-100 trams. Training of the first bus drivers, from Clapham and Wandsworth Depots, started in June 1950.

The two sub-committees dealing with traffic and staff respectively, met every three weeks under the chairmanship of Mr J. B. Burnell, Operating Manager Central Road Services. Details of the changeover to buses were reviewed, with special reference to the readiness of buildings. Tram stop signs were usually removed and replaced by temporary stops at least a week before conversion. Each of the early conversions called for the installation of about 100 new bus stop signs, which were erected in advance and covered with hoods. Since tram stops at road junctions were usually situated immediately before traffic lights in each direction of travel, stops at such places were considerably set back in the interest of traffic flow. Even intermediate stop signs and posts were removed to be replaced by London Transport's standard 'air-foil' design of post and sign.

The re-allocation of cars between depots during the last three years of operation meant that some new route number stencils, with numerals of a more angular design, had to be used on some cars of E/3, 500 series E/1, and ex-Walthamstow Corporation

SPECIAL
WESTMINSTER
ELEPHANT & CASTLE
ST GEORGES CH
BLACKFRIARS
VIA STREATHAM
TOOTING BDWY
VIA CLAPHAM
MARIUS RD
CLAPHAM SOUTH STN
STOCKWELL STN
KENNINGTON
BRIXTON
STREATHAM
SOUTHCROFT RD
WIMBLEDON
VIA TOOTING
MERTON
VIA KENNINGTON & WESTR
EMBANKMENT
VIA ELEPHANT & BLCKFRS
WORKMAN
DEPOT
CLAPHAM
COMMON STN
STREATHAM TOOTING
VIA BRIXTON
TOOTING STREATHAM
VIA CLAPHAM
VICTORIA
VIA STREATHAM
TOOTING AMEN CR
VIA CLAPHAM
CITY & SOUTHWARK
BRIXTON RD

types. The new type stencils were to be seen on routes 12, 22, 24, 34, 36, 38, 46, 54 and 74. The distinctive style of stencil used by Croydon Corporation for their 1926-27 bogie cars lasted to the end of route 16/18 in 1951; some route 18 stencils were converted into a somewhat asymmetric 48. Tramcar indicator blinds were very comprehensive, some having more than 30 indications. The lettering of blinds and side route boards remained of LCC style, standard Gill Sans characters never being used as on buses. A peep-hole was provided in the back of the indicator box to the left of and above the driver's head, through which the abbreviated destination with its number could be seen. Thus indication No 25 on the Camberwell Depot blind was 'Goose Green', and No 35 on the New Cross blind 'Southend Vge'.

The most destructive postwar accident occurred on August 23, 1950, when rebuilt E/1 car 1396 on route

Far left: Destination blind as fitted to cars running from Clapham Depot.

Three views of track laying in 'New Street', on the north side of the County Hall Roundabout.

Top left: Trench excavated. (25.3.50)

Centre left: Yokes and track assembled. (30.3.50)

Bottom left: Concreting complete. (7.4.50)

Below: First day of operation over new north side tracks at County Hall: HR/2 car 1874 turning from Westminster Bridge Road into York Road. (11.6.50)

34 ran away on Cedars Road and demolished a shop (and itself) at the Lavender Hill junction. Route 34 was the only remaining belt-line, and nine miles long with a journey time of 60 minutes, although the termini at Blackfriars and Chelsea were only 3½ miles apart. A six-minute peak service was run, but in slack hours cars turned short of Blackfriars at Camberwell Green. In the evening peak southbound cars were often diverted via Borough Road and Lancaster Street, instead of London Road. Soon after emerging into Newington Causeway, where wartime bombs had removed buildings on both sides of the road, a single track one-way line passed behind the Elephant & Castle public house into Walworth Road, passing then under the railway to Holborn Viaduct. At a minor shopping area at Camberwell Gate, the car entered Camberwell Road, but as far as Camberwell the route lay along a wide but depressing road. On the right approaching Camberwell Green, and opposite a small park, was the east entrance to Camberwell Depot: from June 1949 route 34 was worked from this depot instead of from Clapham, so introducing a considerable variety of cars on to the route, including E/3 and HR/2 types. Just south of Camberwell Green the route curved to the right, and the car changed over to a mile-long overhead section as far as Brixton. At Loughborough Junction route 48 branched off to the left by running on the wrong track for a short distance, and at the third railway bridge there was a short piece of single track.

After crossing Brixton Road, having regained the conduit system, there was a short section of single track in Stockwell Road with the unusual double

conduit, making it impossible to reverse cars there. At 'Swan' Stockwell a sharp left curve brought the car into Clapham Road. Clapham Depot was seen on the left just before stopping at the Clapham Common loading island. At the lights the car turned right into Long Road, a tree-lined avenue, with the Common on the left faced by large residences. A right curve brought the car into Cedars Road, again with superior buildings, and a steep gradient led down to Lavender Hill. The route bore left into Lavender Hill, the approach to Clapham Junction begin on a long down-gradient. In curving right into Falcon Road, the tracks splayed wide apart on each side of a central island, before threading a tunnel formed by a succession of bridges carrying the multitude of tracks from Waterloo and Victoria through Clapham Junction. Despite the frequent railway service, the duplicating tramway services were busy. The car turned right again at Princes Head: here reversed the 612 trolleybus to Mitcham, which like route 34 closed on September 30, 1950. Track paving in Battersea Park Road was latterly bad, in contrast to generally good track on the route. At the Latchmere the car bore left into Battersea Bridge Road, where there was a loading island for Blackfriars-bound cars only. The frowsy area since Clapham Junction now left behind, the car

Top right: Track nearing completion in 'New Curved Street', on the south side of County Hall Roundabout. (14.7.50)

Centre right: South side of County Hall Roundabout: pointwork and curve being laid at the junction of Lambeth Palace Road and Westminster Bridge Road. (6.9.50)

Below: First day of operation over the new south side tracks at County Hall: E/3 car 1968 negotiating openwork curve from Westminster Bridge Road into Lambeth Palace Road. (22.10.50)

Above: Feltham car 2159 on the Victoria Embankment at Waterloo Bridge, about to depart for Telford Avenue Depot at the end of the Saturday midday peak hour. (July 1949)

skirted picturesque Old Battersea, and crossed Battersea Bridge, where each track was laid at the kerb. For 400yd the route ran on the north side of the River up to Kings Road, Chelsea. However during the last six months of operation, route 34 cars had to reverse on the south side of the bridge, after it had been damaged by a collier.

On September 28, 1950, two days before the first tramway closure, which included route 26, a car on that route became derailed at the junction of Blackfriars Road and Southwark Street: the incident occurred at 8.09am, but the breakdown gang had already cleared the line 14 minutes later!

A mobile canteen met incoming cars at Penhall Road on each last night of the trams, and buses were provided to take crews home. The first tram replacement bus was RT 1869, which left Wandsworth Garage at 3.46am on October 1 under Driver R. C. Raikes on route 168 (former 26 tram). At first buses had to enter the garage over the old tram traverser.

The construction in 1950 of extensive new conduit tracks to form a one-way traffic scheme at County Hall attracted very little attention at the time either among the press or the public. The press surprisingly missed a heaven-sent chance of browbeating London Transport for wasting money on needless new works at a time when the days of the trams were already numbered, and high-quality managanese steel scarce. However there was method in this madness, for the layout was necessary to abolish conflicting streams of traffic at County Hall, since York Road was to be the main access to the 1951 Festival of Britain. Even before this, serious peak hour traffic jams regularly occurred at the junction of York Road. The north side of the layout (York Road and Addington Street) was in use for just two years, and the southern side for 20 months. It is remarkable that the completion of the tracks, the last entirely new conduit construction in Britain, took place three weeks after the first routes had been closed. The new tracks provided a glaring contrast with average London conduit track, for nowhere else did the cars ride so smoothly, even the pointwork affording steady riding!

With the closure of the Clapham and Tooting routes on January 6, 1951, when nine miles of route were closed, 101 cars mostly seating 73 passengers were displaced, 55 at Clapham and 46 at Telford Avenue. They were replaced by 117 buses, 77 RTLs at Clapham and 40 RTs at Brixton (formerly Telford Avenue): these buses had only 56 seats, a drop in capacity of over 11%. Brixton was only in partial use, and there were now 127 buses at Clapham. The 230 tram crews were replaced by 253 bus crews: the wage differential whereby tram crews had formerly earned 4/- (20p) a week less than bus crews, was abolished by giving tram men 2/- a week more from January 1, 1951, and a further 2/- from January 1, 1952.

The gossip column of the *Balham, Tooting & Streatham News & Mercury* carried an interesting

Top right: E/3 car 1930 at Defoe Road, Tooting terminus. (3.7.49)

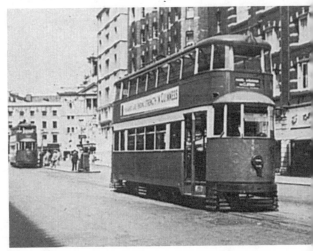

Centre right: Victoria terminus, with Feltham car 2162. (4.6.50)

Below: Ex-Croydon Corporation car 395 approaching Streatham, Gleneagle Road change-pit from the north. (7.1.51)

contribution just after the last cars had run to Tooting. The sympathetic note was unusual, and caught something of the spirit of tram travel. The sentiments expressed, here in shortened form, would now be viewed in the more favourable light of nostalgia:

'It is with the deepest regret that I confess I was prevented from joining in the last tram jollifications at Tooting Broadway at midnight on Saturday. Midnights have not the attraction for me that they once had, and Tooting Broadway is now not the sparkling centre it was forty years ago.

'It was from the top of a tram that I first saw Tooting Broadway and Mitcham. In my view the front seat on top of a tram is a delectable position to occupy. There is more room for one's head and feet. In the bow window one can imagine oneself on top of the world. When the tram is in a frolicsome mood (which a bus never is), one can imagine oneself on a bucking bronco in Wyoming or on a switchback at Mitcham Fair.

'The thought that I shall never again see or hear a tram at Tooting Broadway gives me a pain in the heart. Be hanged to your buses and underground railways! What friendliness is there in them, what romance?

'Trams have always been the salvation of the souls and bodies that work in Fleet Street, and rest from their labours in Mitcham and Tooting. Nearly every morning for years, I heard the cocks of Tooting crowing a welcome to the dawn at Tooting Broadway, and saw the sunrise occasionally from the lighthouse top a tramcar.

'Only in a tram can one savour fellow passengers with the eye of a connoisseur. One can talk splendidly in a tram all the time, intermittently in a bus, and rarely in a tube. A colleague of mine once changed his socks on the top of a tram crossing Mitcham Common. He said his fellow passengers were too enchanted with the view to notice the one he offered".

According to one eye-witness, one Thornton Heath crew never failed in their method of going past Streatham change-pit non-stop! The conductor rode down the hill on the bumper with the trolley rope slack. As he unhooked the pole and raised it to the wire, the driver switched out the controller, using the key to operate the changeover switch, and was ready to apply power again as soon as the conductor rang the bell. There was therefore justification in the display of a request stop at this point.

The first Feltham cars had entered service at the beginning of 1931, the design being far ahead of its time, and ideally suited to London conditions. There was passenger-flow on both decks by way of a front exit (later disused). Large vestibules were provided for standing passengers, and the driver had a separate cab with seat. The cars were so well designed as regards interior appointments and outward appearance, that they could still be termed 'modern' a quarter of a century later. Later claims that the cars were sluggish were not borne out by their performance in London under favourable traffic conditions.

The conversion of the Croydon routes in April 1951 was important inasmuch as by far the longest section

Below: Feltham car 2070 reversing at Norbury on a Saturday morning short working. (2.9.50)

PURLEY - CROYDON - EMBANKMENT — TRAM 16, 18

Service interval : WEEKDAYS before 7 30 a.m., 6 mins., after 7 30 a.m., 3-5 mins.

	WEEKDAYS First					MON. to FRI Last					SATURDAY Last				
	¶¶	†	*	†				†			*		†		
PURLEY *Tram Terminus*	...	...	...	5 37	5 59	10 12	10 23	11 20	....	....	10 9	10 21	11 24	....	....
SOUTH CROYDON *Red Deer*	..	4 41	5 2	5 43	6 5	10 18	10 29	11 26	....	..	10 15	10 27	11 30	....	....
THORNTON HEATH *Pond*		4 58	5 19	6 0	6 22	10 34	10 45	11 42	11 56		10 32	10 44	11 47	11 56	
NORBURY	4 6	5 6	5 27	6 8	6 30	10 42	10 53	11 50	12 4		10 40	10 52	11 55	12 4	
Streatham *St. Leonards Church*	4 12	5 12	5 33	6 14	6 36	10 49	11 0	11 57	12 11		10 46	10 58	12 1	12 10	
Telford Avenue	4 17	5 17	5 38	6 19	6 41	10 54	11 5	12 2	12 16		10 51	11 3	12 6	12 15	
Kennington Gate	4 32	5 34	5 55	6 36	6 58	11 10	11 21				11 9	11 21			
Elephant & Castle			6 1		7 4	11 15					11 15				
Blackfriars *John Carpenter Street*			6 9		7 13	11 24					11 25				
Embankment *Savoy Street*	4 47	5 47	6 12	6 49	7 15	11 27	11 35				11 28	11 35			

	WEEKDAYS First					MON. to FRI Last					SATURDAY Last			
			*	†		*	†		†		*	†		†
Embankment *Savoy Street*		...	4 47	5 46	9 59	10 0	11 27	11 35			10 4	10 2	11 28	11 35
Blackfriars *John Carpenter Street*		...	4 51		..	10 3	..	11 38			..	10 5	..	11 38
Elephant & Castle			4 59			10 12		11 47				10 15		11 48
Kennington Gate			5 5	6 1	10 13	10 17	11 41	11 52			10 18	10 21	11 42	11 52
Telford Avenue	3 51	4 42	5 22	6 18	10 29	10 33	11 57	12 8			10 36	10 39	12 0	12 12
Streatham *St. Leonards Church*	3 56	4 47	5 27	6 23	10 34	10 38	12 2	12 13			10 41	10 44	12 5	12 17
NORBURY	4 2	4 53	5 33	6 29	10 41	10 45	12 9	12 20			10 47	10 50	12 11	12 23
THORNTON HEATH		4 22	5 1	5 41	6 37	10 49	10 53	12 17	12 28		10 55	10 58	12 19	12 31
SOUTH CROYDON *Red Deer*		4 39	5 18	5 58	6 54	11 5	11 9				11 13	11 16		
PURLEY *Tram Terminus*			5 24	6 4	7 0	11 11	11 15				11 19	11 22		

*—Via Blackfriars. †—Via Westminster. ¶—Special early journey.

LATE JOURNEYS—MONDAY to FRIDAY

Croydon *Greyhound* to Streatham *Change Pit* at 1 44 a.m.
Thornton Heath *Pond* to Embankment, via Westminster, at 11 45 p.m.

Embankment to Croydon *Greyhound*, via Blackfriars at 12 35 a.m.
Streatham *Change Pit* to Thornton Heath *Pond* at 2 11 a.m.

PURLEY - CROYDON - EMBANKMENT — TRAM 16, 18

Service interval : SUNDAY 4 minutes.

	SUNDAY First							SUNDAY Last			
	¶	*	†	*	†		†		*	†	
PURLEY *Tram Terminus*						7 35	8 5	....	10 14	10 24	11 20
SOUTH CROYDON *Red Deer*			7 9		7 41	8 11		..	10 20	10 32	11 26
THORNTON HEATH *Pond*	6 9	7 0		7 25	7 33	7 57	8 26		10 35	10 45	11 41 11 58
NORBURY	6 17	7 8	7 25	7 33	7 41	8 5	8 34		10 43	10 53	11 49 12 6
Streatham *St. Leonards Church*	6 24	7 15	7 32	7 40	7 48	8 12	8 41		10 49	10 59	11 55 12 12
Telford Avenue	6 29	7 20	7 37	7 45	7 53	8 17	8 47		10 54	11 4	12 0 12 17
Kennington Gate			7 35	7 52	8 0	8 8	8 32	9 1	11 10	11 20	
Elephant & Castle			7 40		8 5		8 37		11 15		
Blackfriars *John Carpenter Street*			7 48		8 13		8 45		11 24		
Embankment *Savoy Street*		7 51	8 5	8 16	8 21	8 48	9 14		11 27	11 34	

	SUNDAY First						SUNDAY Last				
		*	†	*	†		*	†		†	
Embankment *Savoy Street*				7 45	7 51	8 16	9 59	10 6	11 27	11 35	
Blackfriars *John Carpenter Street*				7 5	7 48	..	10 2	..	11 38		
Elephant & Castle				7 7	7 13	7 56	10 11		11 47		
Kennington Gate			7 12	7 18	8 1	8 4	8 29	10 16	10 20	11 41	11 52
Telford Avenue	6 31		7 22	7 27	7 33	7 6	8 19	8 44	10 32	10 36	11 57 12 8
Streatham *St. Leonards Church*	6 36		7 27	7 32	7 38	8 21	8 24	8 49	10 37	10 41	12 2 12 13
NORBURY	6 43		7 34	7 39	7 45	8 28	8 31	8 56	10 43	10 47	12 8 12 19
THORNTON HEATH *Pond*	6 51	7 12	7 42	7 47	7 53	8 36	8 39	9 4	10 51	10 55	12 16 12 27
SOUTH CROYDON *Red Deer*	7 7	7 27	7 57	8 3	8 8	8 51		9 19	11 6	11 10	
PURLEY *Tram Terminus*		7 33	8 3		8 14	8 57		9 25	11 12	11 16	

*—Via Blackfriars. †—Via Westminster. ¶—Special early journey.

SPECIAL EARLY JOURNEYS—SUNDAY

Croydon *Surrey St.* to Thornton Heath *Pond* at 5 41 a.m.
Thornton H. *Pond* to Streatham *Change Pit* at 5 0 a.m.

Streatham *Change Pit* to Croydon *Surrey Street* at 5 17 a.m.

LATE JOURNEYS—SUNDAY

Croydon *Greyhound* to Streatham *Change Pit* at 1 44 a.m.
Thornton Heath *Pond* to Embankment, via Westminster, at 11 45 p.m.

Embankment to Croydon *Greyhound*, via Blackfriars, at 12 35 a.m.
Streatham *Change Pit* to Thornton Heath *Pond* at 2 11 a.m.

CROYDON - THORNTON HEATH — TRAM 42

Service interval : WEEKDAYS 3-4 mins. (evening 5 mins.), SUNDAY morning 7 minutes (before 9 a.m. 15 mins.), afternoon and evening 5 mins.

	WEEKDAYS First	WEEKDAYS Last		SUNDAY First	SUNDAY Last	
CROYDON *High Street, Coombe Road*	....	5 51	11 33	....	7 20	11 33 ....
WEST CROYDON *Station*	...	5 56	11 38 ..		7 25	11 38 ..
THORNTON HEATH *Pond*	5 21	6 4	11 46 ..	6 51	7 33	11 46 ..
THORNTON HEATH *Whitehorse Road*	5 28	6 11	11 53 ..	6 58	7 40	11 53 ..
THORNTON HEATH *Whitehorse Road*	5 31	....	11 13 11 55	7 0	..	11 13 11 55
THORNTON HEATH *Pond*	5 38	....	11 20 12 2	7 7	..	11 20 12 2
WEST CROYDON *Station*	5 46	..	11 28	7 15	..	11 28
CROYDON *High Street, Coombe Road*	5 51	..	11 33	7 20	..	11 33

Above: Southwark Bridge terminus, with HR/2 car 1860. (17.7.51)

Centre left: Ex-Croydon Corporation car 391 in Brigstock Road at Fire station. (24.3.51)

Bottom left: Ex-Croydon Corporation car 390 in Brigstock Road at Thornton Heath Pond. (7.4.50)

Far left: The London Transport timetables of route 16, 18 and 42 for December 1948./*LTE*.

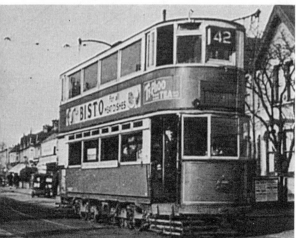

of continuous overhead was closed, and that the remaining Feltham cars were withdrawn. Thus for the last 15 months of the London tramways no modern cars were in service. The Felthams had been used only on routes 8, 10, 16, 18, 20, 22 and 24, since Telford Avenue Depot alone could accommodate them. Regrettable also at this stage was the abandonment of some of the best track in London, that through Croydon. Between Brixton and the centre of Croydon, the cars were well loaded all day, while between Swan and Sugar Loaf (South Croydon) and Purley running was very fast.

New Cross Depot was already being rebuilt early in 1951, although no services running from there had at that time been converted. News that a second entrance was planned in Pepys Road, described at a Deptford Council meeting as 'the best road in the Borough', brought protests from the Council and local people. London Transport promised that the entrance would be unobtrusive, and that no buses would park outside private houses. Conversion of the depot was not finished until after the last London trams ran; it then became the largest garage, with covered space for 300 buses. Rebuilding of Abbey Wood Depot was proceeding in June 1951.

As abandonment proceeded, Rye Lane Permanent Way Yard was given up for garaging buses, and a new permanent way yard built in Old Kent Road, for track maintenance and lifting of disused tracks. On sections due for closing, maintenance did not decline noticeably below prevailing standards, which were tolerably good, although loose mechanical joints were then the norm. Much track was relaid after World War II, this

Top: Victoria Embankment, Blackfriars, with HR/2 car 120 at the western shelter. (2.4.51)

Above: HR/2 car 136 at Peckham Rye terminus. (16.9.51)

Top right: E/1 car 1005 at Camberwell Green. (3.6.50)

Right: Victoria Embankment, Charing Cross, with E/3 car 1966 at the Festival Footbridge. (24.2.52)

work reaching a peak in 1948, when 5½% of the system was relaid, but as was common on British tramways, without renewing the track bed. None of the relaid track was in use for much over five years, against a probable life of about 20 years under London conditions, thus this was obviously a most uneconomic activity. Track failures were not common, if one excepts trouble with conduit point tongues, where ploughs sometimes jammed.

A luckily rare runaway accident occurred on July 2, 1951, when a route 54 car descending the steep incline of Lewisham Way got out of control and ran into a 66, which was standing at the junction of Malpas Road. The 66 in turn struck a 74, which careered on for 100yd from the force of the collision, although the brakes had been fully applied, and the pointsman jumped for his life. Twenty-three persons were injured in the accident.

On April 1, 1952 it was anounced that the last trams would run on July 5, instead of in October as originally planned, when 36 and 38 were to have been the last routes. Four days later routes 33 and 35 were withdrawn, and the Kingsway Subway, showpiece of the London tramways, closed to traffic. At that time it was still one of the very few tramway subways in the world. Even London Transport could not claim that its closure was an 'improvement', and the press suddenly realised that *here* assets were being wasted. A contemporary proposal that a shuttle service could have been retained between Holborn and Westminster was quite practicable, and this would have afforded a short but traffic-free link. Objections to the Subway cars interrupting traffic flow at Waterloo Bridge could

have been overcome by intelligent advance signalling of the cars; in any case traffic lights interrupted the main traffic flow at other points on the Embankment, and there the trams were not to blame. For many years the Kingsway Subway remained as a sad monument to the long departed trams, until it was at length partially utilised as a Strand underpass. On April 5 also the last of the steady-running 100 series HR/2 cars were withdrawn, since they had no trolley poles, and 35 was the last all-conduit route.

London Transport's publicity succeeded in attracting to the trams in their last week of operation vast crowds, who had previously never taken the least interest in this form of transport. The Last Day was certainly a day to avoid for those who wished to sample the trams in comfort for the last time. Suffice it to say that on July 5, 1952, cars were steadily run out of service, apparently for operating convenience, regardless of the fact that far more people than usual were waiting for them on route! The last cars did not actually run into the scrap yard at Penhall Road until the small hours of July 6: then it could truly be said that the London Tram, evidently to the relief of most people, was gone for ever.

Routes 6, 22, 24, 28, 48 and 52 had no direct replacing bus service. Of these 28 and 48 had run

Above: Victoria Embankment at the RAF Memorial, with E/3 car 1987. (10.5.52)

Right: E/1 car 2 at the eastern shelter on the Victoria Embankment at Blackfriars. (26.6.52)

daily, but the others in peak hours only. The 8/20 replacement was no longer a circular, the 181 bus running to Streatham via Tooting, and the 57 to Tooting via Streatham. The 72 was not replaced between Savoy Street and Lewisham, being diverted at the latter point to Crystal Palace. The Brockley Rise to Forest Hill portion of route 66, Blackfriars to London Bridge (26), and Holborn Hall to Agricultural Hall (31) were not replaced, the latter being diverted to Hackney. On the other hand the bus replacement for route 70 was extended from London Bridge to Waterloo, and that for route 34 from Blackfriars to Farringdon Street, and from Battersea Bridge to South Kensington.

Above: Lee change-pit at Leyland Road, with E/3 car 1934. (28.6.52)

In few cities can the outward signs of the trams have disappeared so quickly as in London. The tracks were generally lifted within months of the service ceasing, so that a few months after the last car had run there was little trace of a once-great tramway network. It was obviously difficult to tar over the centre slot, with the hollow conduit below, and this may have speeded the decision to lift the tracks. There was no financial incentive in track-lifting, since the work cost more than could be recovered from the sale of scrap. Thus there was no question that the last traces of the trams were removed for other than practical reasons. In any case local councils had only been waiting for the trams to stop running, in order to reconstruct the roads, and restore levels sadly disturbed by sunken tracks. In this they were encouraged by not having to pay the full cost, since London Transport was obliged to pay its share of road reinstatement.

Two elderly gentlemen, shaky on their legs, but indomitable in spirit, crossed the road:

'Missed us again,' said one briskly as they reached the kerb.

'Ah,' said the other, raising his stick to a passing cyclist.

'We got rid of the trams, now we've got to get rid of the buses!'

26

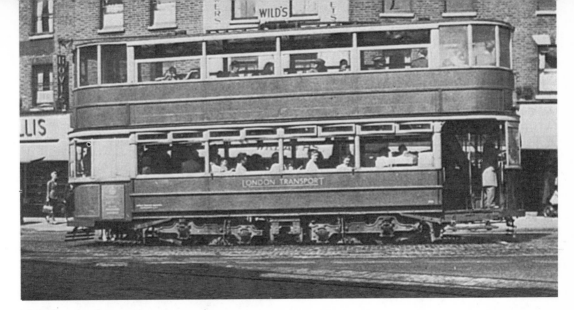

Last Day of the London Trams

Above: Ex-West Ham Corporation car 305 in Old Kent Road at New Cross Gate. (5.7.52)

Centre left: Ex-West Ham Corporation car 297 with slogans on the side at Abbey Wood terminus. (5.7.52)

Bottom left: These long-disused horse tram tracks at Queens Road, Peckham station remained in place long after most of the electric tram tracks had disappeared! (July 1956)

The Swansea and Mumbles Railway

A number of historical records could be claimed by the Swansea & Mumbles Railway. Originally opened in 1804 for mineral traffic as the Oystermouth Railway, with horses as motive power, it became in 1807 the first railway in the world to carry fare-paying passengers. Steam traction was not introduced until 1877, and when the line assumed its final form with an extension to Mumbles Pier in 1898, the Oystermouth to Black Pill section was re-aligned. In 1929 it became the last complete tramway in Britain to be electrified, being operated by the South Wales Transport Co. When it was closed on January 5, 1960, electric tramway operation in Wales ceased.

The standard-gauge line was on private right of way, which was laid with Vignoles rail, the wheels of the cars being of railway profile (tramcar wheels usually have a flange no more than ½in deep and a much narrower tyre). This enabled check rails to be dispensed with throughout, in spite of the use of double deck cars. However the line was usually considered to be a tramway by dint of the type of vehicle used and the method of operation, whereby there was signalling only at the loops. Otherwise the 5½-mile long line was mainly single track, which was situated at the roadside at the Swansea end, giving way to private track near the shore towards the Mumbles. The infrequent stops, at about half-mile intervals, permitted a fairly brisk run. Ribbon development accompanied the line intermittently for most of its length, and at no point did it become rural, but on the outer section the view was partly open toward the northern hills. The line was virtually free of gradients, being close to sea level for the whole distance. At Mumbles Pier there were queueing arrangements, for at fine weekends the cars were very busy with trippers bound for the picturesque Gower Peninsula.

The 13 cars were all alike, two having been added in 1930. Their seating capacity of 106 was unsurpassed by any other British tramcar. At 45ft these cars were some of the longest ever built for a British tramway, but the motormen's cabs were very small. The cars had two motors each, were equipped with electric and air brakes, and were able to run coupled in pairs, a feature never adopted as standard practice by any other British system. The unusual pantograph current collector was found elsewhere only at Sunderland as a standard fitting. The colour scheme was red with a cream band. The curious arrangement of entrances on the landward side only was occasioned by the fact that the line ran very close to the sea near the Mumbles.

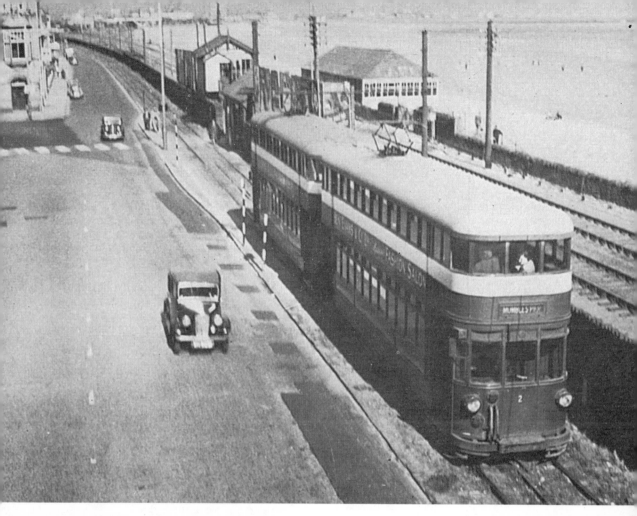

Far left: Rutland Street Depot, Swansea, with cars 7 and 11. The wide track grooves to accommodate railway type wheels can be clearly seen. (4.9.55)

Above: Train bound for Mumbles Pier at St Helens, headed by car 2. (18.5.57)

Left: Mumbles Pier terminus, looking across Swansea Bay, with car 7. (4.9.55)

Birmingham

By far the largest 3ft 6in gauge system in Britain, Birmingham was also the last, apart from Llandudno. The maximum route mileage was 80½.

The first horse tramway in Birmingham was opened in 1873. Steam trams ran from 1882 to 1906, the network being quite extensive. The Hockley and Handsworth route was served by cable cars from 1888 to 1911, and battery cars ran for a number of years on the Bournebrook route.

The Bournebrook route also saw the first electric cars in 1901. The first electric lines were worked by the City of Birmingham Tramways Co Ltd, which was taken over by Birmingham Corporation in 1907-12. The Steelhouse Lane group of routes as far as Aston were the first to be worked by the Corporation, in 1904.

A progressive policy was followed as regards the layout of routes, the first reserved track being opened in 1919 in Pebble Mill Road. The extension from Selly Oak to Longbridge was built in 1923 mainly on reservation, the branches to Rednal and Rubery being opened in 1924 and 1926 respectively. The total length of reservation between Selly Oak and Rednal and Rubery was nearly six miles. Some sections were improved by removing street track to reservation, as with the outer end of the Washwood Heath route. The last new extension to be opened was that to Fort Dunlop in 1930. However as late as 1938 the street line through Erdington was replaced by a reserved track by-pass, this being the last new construction. Between 1924 and 1939 Birmingham cars operated beyond the City boundary to Dudley and Wednesbury.

Below: Navigation Street terminus, departure point for routes to Rednal and Rubery, with car 798 in foreground. (29.6.52)

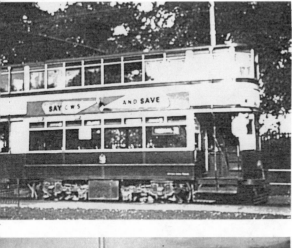

Above: Rubery terminus in Bristol Road South, with ornamental shelter. (29.6.52)

Centre left: Former bow-collector car at Rednal terminus. (1.7.51)

Bottom left: Burnley truck on the above car. (1.7.51)

A peculiarity of the system was that there were no through routes across the central area, but instead a number of termini of the periphery as in London. Central termini were at one time situated at Edmund Street, Snow Hill, Steelhouse Lane, Martineau Street, Albert Street, Navigation Street and Hill Street.

The south-eastern routes from Leopold Street to Cannon Hill and Alcester Lanes End made extensive use of one-way streets. The line from Selly Oak to Rednal and Rubery was entirely reservation except for half a mile at Northfield. The main workday traffic came from the Austin Works at Longbridge. At weekends there was heavy excursion traffic to Rednal, where there were special loading arrangements, as well as the only turning circle on the system.

Above: Car 716 at Gravelly Hill. (17.9.50)

Right: Pype Hayes Park terminus, with car 647. (1.7.51)

Far right, top: Car 776 turning short of Washwood Heath terminus. The final section is occupied by bow-collector cars parked during the conversion of Washwood Heath Depot to bus operation. (17.9.50)

Far right, bottom: Car 405 at Alcester Lanes End terminus. (25.9.49)

The northern routes based on Steelhouse Lane terminus had a very high proportion of reserved track. The three branches to Erdington, Short Heath and Pype Hayes Park diverged at Gravelly Hill, from which point the Pype Hayes Park route was wholly on reservation (2½ miles). On the latter line was also the Fort Dunlop branch, served only by works specials. Erdington and Pype Hayes Park had a six minute service, and Short Heath an eight minute service.

The Washwood Heath and Alum Rock routes ran from Martineau Street terminus. These routes (and earlier that to Lodge Road) were arranged for bow-collector cars, all other routes on the system being worked by cars with trolley poles.

Birmingham cars were very conventional, and to the uninitiated at least, not of great variety, being conveniently divided into four-wheel and bogie cars. The bogie cars had only 62 seats, because the top deck seating was two and one transverse, due to the narrowness of the cars.

The last four-wheel cars, Nos 401-450, ran from

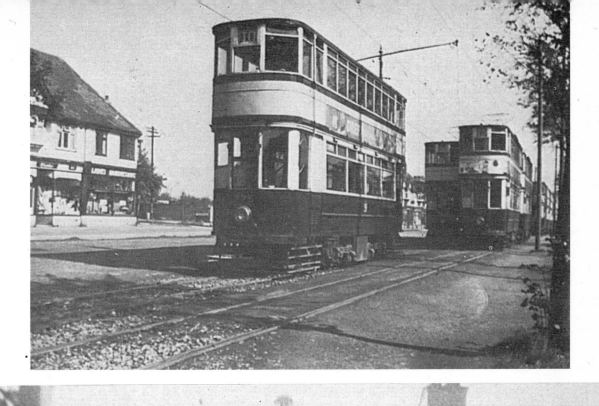

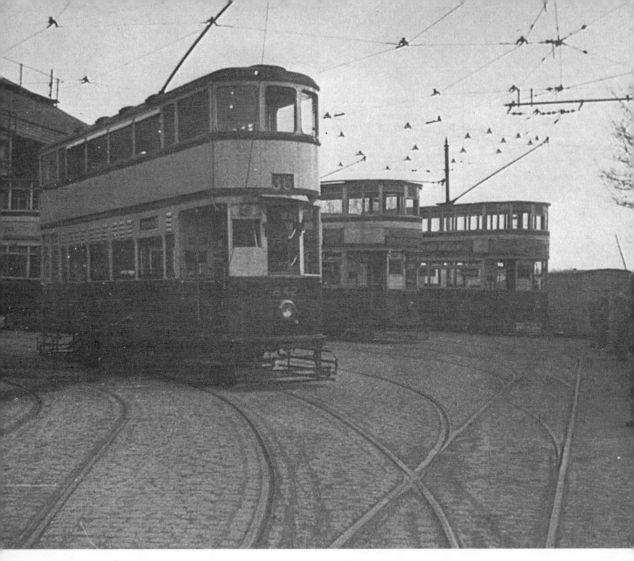

Above: Cars 842, 818 and 739 (from left to right) in Cotteridge Depot yard. (20.4.52)

Right: Bow-collector car 778 at Alum Rock terminus. (25.9.49)

Far right: Car 842 in Cotteridge Depot yard. (20.4.52)

Moseley Road Depot, and were withdrawn in 1949 after closure of the Alcester Lanes End route. They were built in 1912-13, had air-oil brakes and two 40hp motors, and seated 54 passengers.

Originally having open balconies, Nos 587-636 were built in 1920-21. These cars were 16ft 0½in high, which made them taller than the London standard cars, despite the narrow gauge.

Nos 762-811 were built in 1928 and had 63hp motors as the previous type. The cars were fitted with bow collectors, and had eight windows a side on the top deck.

The only modern cars were Nos 842 and 843, built in 1929 and 1930 respectively. Both had 40hp motors, and were the last cars built for the system. It will thus be seen that the development of the tramways stopped short fully 20 years before the final closure.

The running of Birmingham cars was quite brisk, especially on the reserved track sections. The two 63hp motors with which many were fitted made them more powerful (on paper at any rate) than most London cars. An unusual feature retained to the end was the sunblind that could be let down in front of the driver's window, a similar arrangement always having obtained on Swiss cars. The cars were always kept well maintained and clean.

A route number only was carried on the front of the car. A combined destination and route number indicator was displayed in the side window next the entrance. A unique feature of the Birmingham numbering scheme was the use of a separate route number to each short working point; however this and the limited destination information were of little help to the stranger! The livery was navy blue and primrose, and advertisements were always carried.

At one time there were 11 depots. In 1952 depots were situated at Selly Oak (Rednal and Rubery routes), Cotteridge (Cotteridge route), and Miller Street (Erdington, Pype Hayes Park and Short Heath routes). Witton Depot was still in use, and the overhaul works was at Kyott's Lake Road.

The track was well maintained to the end of operation, and contributed greatly to the smooth running of the cars; the freedom from pitching and swaying was all the more remarkable for a narrow gauge tramway.

Fares were quite low. The maximum fare in the early 1950s was 4d (1½p); the single fare from the City to Erdington, Short Heath or Pype Hayes Park in 1951 was 3½d — for up to five miles of travel. The 1949 operating cost of 27.1d (11p) per car mile had been among the highest of any British tramway.

For a large undertaking, the closure of the Birmingham tramways was probably the most drawn out. The Nechells route was replaced by trolleybuses in 1922. Abandonment started in earnest at the time of the Yardley route conversion to trolleybuses in 1934: all other routes were however replaced by motor buses. By 1939 the four south-eastern routes and most of the western routes had ceased operation.

Bow-collector operation ceased in October 1950, with the closure of the routes running from Washwood Heath Depot. By the summer of 1951 the system was reduced to the Navigation Street routes to Cotteridge, Rednal and Rubery, as well as the Steelhouse Lane routes to Erdington, Short Heath and Pype Hayes Park, and the Fort Dunlop branch. It was a measure of the heavy traffic carried that no less than 263 cars were needed for the remaining 27 miles of route, though a high proportion were in use in the peak hour only; the remaining south-east London tramways had a similar route mileage in April-July 1952, but managed with only about 160 cars.

The southern routes closed in 1952, tramway operation ceasing with the abandonment of the northern routes on July 4, 1953.

Leicester

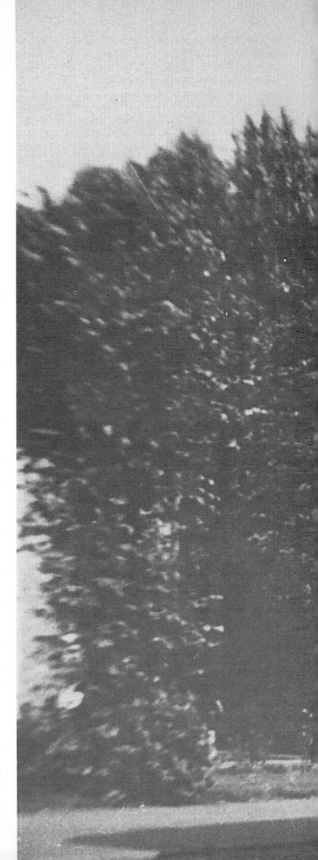

At the height of the tramway period Leicester was noted, in common with several other Midland cities, for its textile, leather and engineering products. A striking feature of the city was its compactness.

A system of horse tramways had operated in Leicester since the 1870s. The first electric route opened in 1904 to Stoneygate, and by 1905 the tramways were virtually complete. The system was originally worked by 140 cars, of which 41 were top covered. Twenty larger cars were delivered in 1913-14, and the final batch of 18 followed in 1920. All 178 cars had four-wheel trucks, mostly of 6ft wheelbase, and open ends, although most cars were later totally enclosed. The colour scheme was always maroon and cream.

There were nearly 23 miles of standard gauge tramway. The network was extremely dense, and radiated from the Clock Tower in the centre. Due to the limited boundaries and absence of ribbon development, most routes came to abrupt end at the limit of building, with in many cases open country beyond. No route was more than three miles long. There were also some cross-connections, and reserved track existed in Blackbird Road and Coleman Road.

Although most of the system was built in 1904-05, some short sections were opened in the 1920s, the last new line being that in Coleman Road, opened in 1927. This latter was one of first to the closed, surviving only until 1938. The single-and-loop Melbourne Road route became the first to be closed in 1933, in which year the routes were numbered 1 to 9, the numbers appearing on the cars.

Right: Stoneygate terminus, with car No 78, which had an upper deck shorter than the lower. (21.8.49)

Depots were situated at Abbey Park (150 cars), and at Humberstone Gate near the centre (25 cars). Until 1925 depots for six cars each existed at Stoneygate and near Narborough Road terminus.

The cars and track were always well maintained, but the system never recovered from the neglect of World War II. As late as 1947 the track layout at the Clock Tower was altered to permit the trams to keep left, in accordance with other traffic. Up to this date, most of the routes were still running.

In August 1949 trams remained only on the Belgrave Road, Humberstone and Stoneygate routes. The last section to be closed was that to Humberstone, on November 9, 1949.

Above: Car 38 at Belgrave Road terminus. (21.8.49)

Top right: Car 21 at Abbey Park Depot. (21.8.49)

Bottom right: The Leyland tower wagon of 1911, still in use in 1949! (21.8.49)

Llandudno and Colwyn Bay Electric Railway

The 3ft 6in gauge tramway, which crossed the boundary between Caernarvonshire and Denbighshire at Penrhyn Bay, was opened in 1907 between West Shore, Llandudno and the depot at Rhos.

In the following year the line was extended to Colwyn Bay, and finally to Old Colwyn in 1915, bringing the length of route open to 8¼ miles. The short West Shore Parade section had fallen into disuse by 1917, while the Old Colwyn extension was abandoned in 1930. This reduced the line to its final layout, with a total mileage of 6½, all but two miles of the route taking the form of a street tramway.

The terminus at Colwyn Bay was in the main shopping centre in Abergele Road at Greenhill Road. After leaving the terminus, a stub in the middle of the road, the line descended slightly, passing shortly beyond over a section of interlaced track. On the bridge over the London Midland Region main line to Holyhead, there was a single track, and here the line described a reverse curve. At the bottom of Whitehall Road, the route turned left along the sea front at Rhos, this being the only coastal section of street track. After a quarter of a mile, the tramway turned inland to reach

The seaside resorts of North Wales are particularly favoured in that they are sheltered from the prevailing winds, have excellent sandy beaches and a hinterland of the glorious Welsh mountains. The area formerly served by the tramway contains the seaside resorts of Llandudno, Rhos-on-Sea and Colwyn Bay, much frequented by visitors from Lancashire, with a resident population of about 40,000. The immediate vicinity is hilly, with the Great Ormes Head rising abruptly to 679ft. When the trams were running, the built-up area was mainly confined to the coast, with open country inland, indeed between Rhos and Llandudno there was merely a thin line of development.

Below: Rhos-on-Sea Depot, with ex-Accrington car 4 (left) and ex-Bournemouth car 8. (27.8.55)

the eight-track depot on the outskirts of Rhos. It was a building of brick construction with a corrugated-iron roof, and also contained the workshops, with the offices adjoining.

A short distance beyond the depot, the paved road came to an end, and there were a few hundred yards of private track in Marine Road beyond, where at Penrhyn Bay the coast was rejoined; at this point single track working was in force during the summer of 1955, while a sea wall was under construction. The line then turned inland along the unmade Glan-y-Mor Road. In the early days it was quite common for electric tramways to run along unpaved roads, but even then the track area was usually paved: this must have been the last example of its kind in Britain. At Penrhyn Hill the steepest gradient of 1:11 was ascended, the sheer rock face of the Little Ormes Head being on the right hand side of the reservation, the first part of which was somewhat above the level of the

Top left: Hawarden Road, Colwyn Bay, with ex-Accrington car 3. (5.10.51)

Centre left: Colwyn Bay terminus, with ex-Bournemouth car 7. (30.9.51)

Below: Interior of the west shed at Rhos-on-Sea, with (from left to right) cars 17 and 20, ex-Bournemouth car 6, and a works car. (27.8.55)

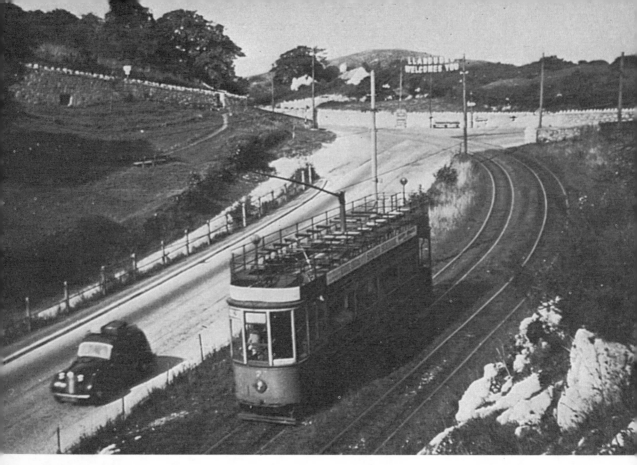

parallel road. After a short down gradient on street track, Craigside was reached, where there was a clear view across a wedge of countryside toward Llandudno. The neat private right of way across Bodafon Fields extended as far as Craig-y-Don. The trams traversed a mile of street track through the main shopping centre of Llandudno before reaching Palladium Corner in the town centre, the last section being single track; the stops at Palladium Corner however were situated on a loop. Llandudno preserves much of its Edwardian atmosphere in the form of the unusual colonnaded shop fronts, notably in Mostyn Street. A sharp left curve brought the line to the West Shore terminus via Gloddaeth Avenue, where there was also single track apart from one loop, the terminus taking the form of a stub.

The journey time latterly was 43 minutes, reduced to 40 minutes in winter, with two minutes layover at each end, the round trip thus taking 90 minutes. During the last winter of operation, the basic service was 20 minutes on weekdays, but only a half-hourly service was provided between Rhos Depot and Colwyn Bay on Sundays, the remainder of the line being unserved. The through fare was 9d (4p) at the time of closure.

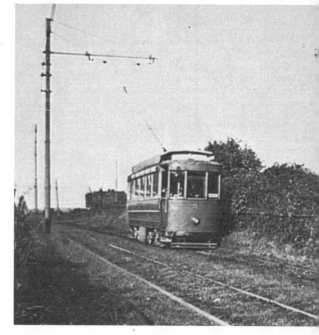

Top left: Penrhyn Hill, Little Ormes Head, with ex-Bournemouth car 7. (30.9.51)

Left: Private right of way across open fields between Craig-y-Don and Little Orme with ex-Accrington car 2, one of two with original trucks. (5.10.51)

Above: The end of the private right of way at Craig-y-Don, with car 22. The Little Orme is seen in the distance. (27.8.55)

The pride of the fleet were the ex-Darwen cars 23 and 24, built in 1936-37 for the 4ft gauge, and bought in 1946. These fine vehicles were the only really modern cars ever built for the narrow gauge, being similar to the Blackpool cars of the same period, but narrower. There was luxurious two-and-one seating on both decks and a cab for the driver. The cars entered service in 1948, and were used for shuttle services at both ends of the line, latterly however on the Colwyn Bay section only. Permission could not be obtained for their use over the whole of the line, because of the exposed nature of the Penrhyn Bay section. The riding was very steady and smooth, as a ride in 1951 proved.

between Rhos Depot and Colwyn Bay terminus proved.

The ex-Bournemouth cars were bought in 1936, car 6 dating from 1914, the others having been built between 1921 and 1926 to long obsolete designs! They had longitudinal upholstered seats in the lower deck and transverse wooden seating upstairs, giving a total of 66. The cars tended to be sluggish, the two 40hp motors with which most of them were fitted giving a top speed of barely 25mph. All 23 cars in the fleet were painted apple green and cream. The coat of arms consisted of a dragon on a shield encircled by the words *Llandudno and Colwyn Bay Electric Railway Limited.*

In the last decade of operation, the track received much attention, and the riding of the cars was quite good, but this may have been partly due to the low average speeds. This was the last privately-owned street tramway in the British Isles, and the last to work open top cars. The writer remembers vividly a return journey on such a car from Llandudno to Colwyn Bay one autumn evening in 1951. The exhilarating coolness of the breeze and the rhythmic swaying of the car travelling through the darkness at its comfortable pace is an experience not easily forgotten.

The line was forced to close by the generally high costs experienced by tramway undertakings, aggravated by expenses for sea defence works at Penrhyn Bay, where a good deal of erosion occurred in the winters of 1948-49 and 1952-53. The decision to close was taken reluctantly, and the Company kept going for longer than could have been expected. The Urban District Councils of Llandudno and Colwyn Bay did not consider the expense of saving the line to be justified, not even on amenity grounds in a holiday district. Ex-Bournemouth car 8 was the last in service: it arrived at Rhos Depot at 12.11am on March 25, 1956.

Above: Mostyn Street, Llandudno, with ex-Accrington car 5, one of two with original trucks. (5.10.51)

Top right: Ex-Bournemouth car 10 and ex-Accrington car 5 passing on Palladium Corner loop, Llandudno. (5.10.51)

Centre right: West Shore terminus, Llandudno, with ex-Bournemouth car 10. (30.9.51)

Bottom right: Ex-Bournemouth car at West Shore terminus. (27.8.55)

44

Howth

on private track, the entire route being single track and loop, and mostly laid with Vignoles rail.

The ten cars were all similar. No 1-8 were built by Brush, seated 67 passengers and were in blue and white livery. The two cars in natural teak finish, Nos 9 and 10, were built by Milnes, and were slightly longer than the others, seating 72.

The line was latterly owned by Coras Iompair Eireann (Irish Transport Company). Abandonment was mooted in 1955, but was delayed by the need to build a new road. The line closed on May 31, 1959; it was the last tramway in the world to be run entirely with open-top double deckers, and the last electric rail transport in Ireland.

The peninsula of Howth Head is situated some eight miles east of Dublin, and forms the northern limit of Dublin Bay. In 1901 the Great Northern Railway of Ireland opened a 5ft 3in gauge line between Sutton and Howth Station via Howth Summit, a distance of 5½ miles. This line described a semi-circle round the south of the promontory, the fine views thus afforded making it one of the most scenic rides of any tramway in the British Isles. There were some fair gradients, including a 1:16 descent from the Summit at Howth, which was 350ft above sea level. About half the line was in the form of a roadside reservation, and the rest

Below: Car 7 at Howth Summit. (29.8.55)

Top right: The junction of Strand Road and Carrick Brack Road, near Sutton, with car 8. (14.6.53)

Bottom right: Cars 1 and 3 (foreground) in Sutton Depot. (29.8.55)

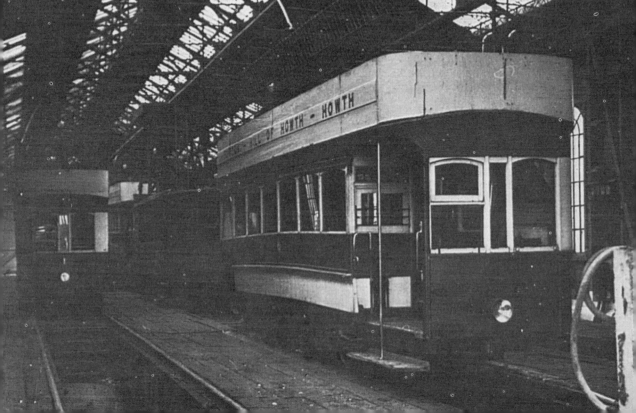

Liverpool

Horse cars started running in 1869 between Exchange and Dingle. By 1895 there were 267 cars serving 68 miles of track. In 1897 the Corporation took over the system and started electrification, the first electric line being opened between South Castle Street and Dingle in 1898. The rolling stock for this line consisted of 15 German-built four-wheel motors and trailers similar to those in use in Hamburg, 12 American-type bogie single deckers, and three American double deckers.

Route numbers were first displayed in 1913, and in the latter-day display were very prominent, together with informative destination indicators. The first reserved track line was completed to Bowring Park in 1915. Early reservations were conversions of street track, but extensions constructed after World War I were built mainly as central or side reservation along generously laid out roads. The outer three miles of the Prescot route had formerly been privately owned, but were taken over by Liverpool in 1919, and converted to reserved track. Although the track connected with the St Helens tramways, there was no regular through working.

Most of the central area routes terminated at the Pierhead, where there were three turning circles. There the cars connected with the Birkenhead Ferries. The central streets were generally wide and the tramway layout very comprehensive, but there were few loading islands. The system as a whole had little single track. The routes to the north served the poorest areas, but the tramways were extended to keep pace with the rapid expansion of the City in the 1920s and 1930s, and here (rarely in British transport planning) provision was made for the trams in advance. Thus in Liverpool the trams did not cause much delay to motor traffic.

Edge Lane Works was opened in 1928, and eventually employed up to 1,000 workers. Nearly all the large fleet of cars built subsequently originated here. Up to 1930 the fleet was composed mostly of four-wheelers, which had been progressively improved with top covers and modern equipment. They were finally totally enclosed, but unvestibuled cars were still in use in 1946.

Below: St George's Hall from William Brown Street, with bogie streamliner 909. (14.6.56)

Top right: Streamlined four-wheel car 237 at Fazakerley terminus. (9.5.49)

Bottom right: Pierhead terminus, with four-wheeler 747 and bogie car 829, built in 1926-27 and 1935-36 respectively. (1.10.51)

Above: What to do? Car 89 broken down in South Castle Street. (9.5.49)

Right: Streamlined bogie car 990 at Page Moss Avenue. (1.10.51)

In 1931 a great programme of new construction started. Up to 1936 110 bogie cars had been built. They were followed in 1936-37 by 163 streamlined bogie cars, and in 1938-42 by 104 streamlined four-wheel cars. The latter were cheaper to build and more economical in operation, but probably harder on the track due to harsher riding and greater axle loads. The former livery of crimson lake and ivory was changed to olive green and cream from 1933, but from 1946 a brighter green was used. The fleet reached a maximum of 788 cars.

The last extension, that to Kirby, was opened in 1943; with a length of nine miles it was the longest route. Thus the system reached its maximum extent of 98 route miles on standard gauge, of which 28 miles were on reserved track. It was the fourth largest tramway undertaking in Britain, and served by 63 routes.

Nowhere could tramway reserved tracks be seen to more advantage than in Liverpool. The new suburban roads were spaciously laid out, while the reservations ensured that there was no mutual interference between trams and other traffic; at the same time there was no loss of access such as occurs in full railway-type segregation. The turfing of the tracks completed the aesthetic picture.

During World War II the cars and especially the sleeper tracks suffered from want of maintenance, and in November 1945 the City Council endorsed a proposal to abandon the tramways in favour of buses.

Public opposition to the decision existed, but attracted little support, confirming that official decisions of this type were rarely questioned! On November 7, 1947 a fire at Green Lane Depot destroyed 66 streamlined cars, so that the service had to be reduced on each route.

Outer Circle route 26/27 became in 1948 the first to be converted. In the early 1950s 146 streamlined cars were reconstructed to enable them to run until replacing buses could be obtained. By January 1952 one-third of the route mileage had been closed, and more than half the cars disposed of. As each route closed, transfer and workman's fares were withdrawn.

At one time there were depots at Dingle, Edge Lane, Garston, Green Lane, Litherland, Prince Alfred Road, and Walton. Towards the end of operation, the four-wheel streamlined cars were preferred to the bogies, which were withdrawn after damage or defects; many of the bogie cars were sold to Glasgow. The four-wheelers were simpler to maintain and required less current, and provided the whole service from Edge Lane Depot on routes 6A and 40, to Bowring Park and Page Moss Avenue respectively; these routes were the last to run, and closed on September 14, 1957.

Stockport

The large Manchester system was itself but part of an extensive network all on 4ft 8½in gauge, mostly municipally operated, but including the lines of the South Lancashire Tramways Company: Oldham and Salford cars ran through to Manchester until 1946 and 1947 respectively.

The Stockport system was the southernmost outpost and last survivor of the vast tramway network surrounding Manchester, though all the routes were in fact in Cheshire. Horse tramways to Levenshulme, Edgeley and Hazel Grove were running by 1890. The first electric cars ran in 1901, and electrification was completed in 1905, when a joint service of Stockport and Manchester cars started running through from Hazel Grove, the most southerly point on the system, to Manchester.

A joint service was also worked with the Stockport, Hyde, Mossley & Dukinfield Transport & Electricity Board (SHMD) between Stockport and Hyde, but this was cut back to Vernon Park in 1947. Up to this time only a short section of the Stockport tramways, between Cheadle and Gatley, had ever been closed. At their maximum the tramways consisted of 14½ miles of route. The only extensive single track sections were on the Vernon Park route, but the Reddish route also included single line.

The through service to Manchester ceased with the closure of that system in 1949, when the operating cost of Stockport's cars was very high at 26.2d (11p) per mile, or nearly 50% more than its buses. At this

Right: Mersey Square, with the depot in the background, and car 52. (5.6.51)

Top left: Car 52 in Mersey Square. (5.6.51)

Bottom left: Reddish terminus, with car 80. (5.6.51)

Above: Car 59 loading at Princes Street loop, near the town centre. (5.6.51)

period there were 82 cars in service, all four-wheel top covered, 26 cars having open balconies; the livery was red and white. In early 1950 the Vernon Park to Edgeley, and Reddish to Cheadle Heath routes were still running, and some new track was even laid that summer. The tramways were kept in a good state of repair to the end, and were equipped with automatic points and trolley reversers.

The main depot was situated in Mersey Square, the centre of the system, though there was a smaller depot close by at Heaton Lane. At the time of closure on August 25, 1951, trams were confined to the Mersey Square to Reddish route only.

Sheffield

The foremost steel city in Britain also included among its products tramway trackwork, of which Hadfields and Edgar Allen were the leading manufacturers.

The first Sheffield horse trams ran in 1873. In 1899 electric operation was introduced on the route between Tinsley and Nether Edge. The latter was among the only two short sections of route to be closed up to 1952, when there were 48 miles of standard gauge route.

Although loading islands were a feature of the tramways, especially at termini, they were mainly confined to busy points, and most stops in the City centre had carriageway loading. The northbound stop in High Street took the form of a white strip painted on the roadway. Particularly noteworthy were the loading shelters for southbound passengers in Pinstone Street,

served by a third track laid in to the kerb. Short working cars from the north of the City reversed by means of a loop via Church Street and Leopold Street. The centre of Sheffield was not ideal for tramway operation, the busy section between Lady's Bridge and Fitzalan Square being too narrow for the volume of tram and motor traffic.

The northern exit from the centre was by way of Wicker Arches, where there was centre pole construction, and this was the only connection between the northern and southern parts of the network. At the northern end of Wicker Arches, the route to Tinsley kept straight on through a depressing industrial area, where there were several large steelworks. The Vulcan Road terminus at Tinsley consisted of a spur 400yd long. Hadfields Works at the end of the road was the main source of traffic: in the peak hour extra cars ran from here to many parts of the system.

Through cars between Sheffield and Rotherham reversed in the City centre by running in an anti-clockwise direction via Lady's Bridge, Exchange Street and Blank Street. The service was worked jointly by Sheffield and Rotherham cars, the latter being single enders with bodywork similar to a trolleybus. The service was temporarily suspended beyond Tinsley after December 11, 1948, because of

Below: The kerbside loading bay at the Town Hall in Pinstone Street, with Domed-Roof car 231. (25.3.60)

impending reconstruction of bridges at that point, but was never resumed. Rotherham ran a shuttle service to Templeborough for a time, but ceased tramway operation in 1949; it considered that the expense of track reinstatement, after completion of the work at Tinsley, was not justified.

At Hunter's Bar, the junction of the Fullwood and Eccleshall routes, the down and up tracks respectively were joined by a spur to form a turning circle for short workings. The Middlewood and Wadsly Bridge routes ran for most of their length very close together. Some of the routes to the north and north-west had fair gradients, the most severe being on the Walkley route.

Branching off from the Tinsley route just past the Wicker, the Lane Top route climbed steadily to its terminus. This started with a steep climb up Spital Hill, followed by more moderate gradients and a drop at Fir Vale. The pleasant wooded Firth Park flanked the route on both sides on the last section.

In the east, the Intake and Handsworth routes were connected by a reserved track line along Prince of Wales Road, opened in 1928. The Intake route included a mile-long 1:10 gradient.

Top left: The Moor, with Standard car 224. (27.9.52)

Centre left: Houndsfield Road, Western Bank, with Roberts car 529. (24.9.52)

Below: Standard cars 103 (left) and 124 near Walkley terminus. (24.9.52)

On the Beauchief route, alternate cars reversed at Millhouses, where there was a turning circle. Beyond Millhouses, the line took the form of an attractive roadside reservation with tall overhanging trees as far as Beauchief. From there the line in Abbey Lane, opened in 1927, formed a mainly reserved track route to Woodseats. Abbey Lane was generously laid out, and a superior residential area.

At Woodseats a short branch continued to Meadowhead up a steep hill. The return to Sheffield along the Chesterfield Road traversed a depressing area. At Woodbank Crescent however the route followed a road carried on a shelf cut out of the hillside, giving extensive and dramatic views over the south-west part of the City.

Sheffield was most unusual among British tramway operators in having consistently introduced improved cars over the years, a policy which continued down to 1952. The cars were exemplified and their appearance enhanced by curved glass windows at the ends of both decks, and thin window frames giving maximum visibility for passengers and driver; the interior layout was convenient, with comfortable seating. All were built to a standard length of just under 33ft, and were double deckers on four-wheel 8ft 6in wheelbase trucks, though the Roberts cars had 9ft wheelbase trucks.

There were 452 cars in service in April 1951, carrying 175 million passengers a year, or 64% of the traffic, the remainder of which was carried by 372 buses. Only about 75 cars were more than 25 years old.

Between 1928 and 1936 the improved flush-panelled side Standard type was introduced, most of the 200 units being built by the undertaking. These cars indeed set a very high standard for a car of traditional layout, and were much superior to similar cars built elsewhere at the period.

The Domed-Roof cars, while recognisably a typical Sheffield product, were a further improvement, and among the neatest cars of the kind ever built. The undertaking built 65 of them between 1936 and 1939.

During World War II Sheffield was forced by losses through bombing, in which the City centre was badly damaged, to purchase some second hand cars. Thirteen ex-Newcastle cars entered service in 1942. They were followed in 1943 by ten ex-Bradford cars, which first had to be rebuilt, this mainly entailing enclosure of the upper deck balconies before they could enter service: being built for the 4ft gauge and also four-wheelers, these cars were required by the Board of Trade to have open balconies.

Car 501 was the prototype of the Roberts cars, but was built by the undertaking, and appeared in July 1946. The production batch of 35 cars, built by Charles Roberts & Co Ltd, followed in 1950-52. They differed from 501 in having all-metal bodies. The cars had two 65hp motors and folding doors, and were very comfortable and smooth riding. It is a great pity that this excellent design could not be adopted as a standard car for medium-sized tramway systems; as it was Sheffield remained one of the very few cities where one could enjoy a ride on a really modern four-wheel car. Charles Roberts tried unsuccessfully to interest other systems in this type of car. It is possible that

Below: Burngreave Road, with Standard car 79. (24.9.52)

Top right: Standard car 1 on the descent from Lane Top terminus. (21.9.52)

Centre right: Lane Top terminus, with Domed-Roof car 296 (in foreground) and Roberts car 509. (27.2.60)

Bottom right: Abbeydale Road, Beauchief reserved track, with Standard car 113. (21.9.52)

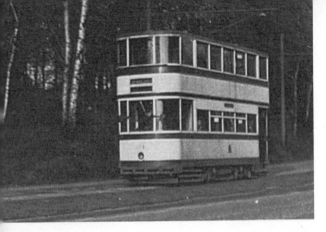

other cities were prejudiced against long-wheelbase four-wheelers, although their operation in Sheffield was most successful.

The hilly nature of the city made it essential to provide the trams with exceptionally effective brakes. The braking system on Sheffield cars was very comprehensive, and was entirely actuated by the controller handle, eliminating the need for an additional lever. The air-wheel brake was used for normal stops, but further retardation was available by moving the brake handle to the higher brake notches, thus activating first the air-track brake (this is turn cutting out the air-wheel brake), and then the rheostatic and magnetic track brakes. An interesting refinement was selective side sanding, involving the use of two pedals, to ensure a good start on curves without risk of derailment; in such a situation sand would be deposited on to the outer rail only.

Until 1936, the upper panels of all cars were painted cream, and the lower navy blue, however on the pre-1928 cars the rocker panel was cream. The Domed-Roof cars introduced an all-over cream livery with

Top left: Abbeydale Road, Beauchief reserved track, with Standard car 174. (27.2.60)

Centre left: Domed-Roof cars near Meadowhead terminus. (15.9.54)

Below: Domed-Roof car 85 (in foreground) and Standard car 69 at Meadowhead terminus. (27.2.60)

Right: Chesterfield Road, Woodseats, with Domed-Roof car 85. (27.2.60)

Above: Car 473, built in 1926-27, at Millhouses. (6.6.51)

Centre right: Standard car 69, built in 1930, at Meadowhead. (27.2.60)

Bottom right: Vulcan Road, Tinsley terminus, with Domed-Roof car 100. This car was built during World War II to the 1936-39 design. (6.6.51)

Far right, top: Roberts car 509, built in 1950, at Lane Top. (27.2.60)

Far right, bottom: Roberts car 527, built in 1950, at Beauchief. (27.2.60)

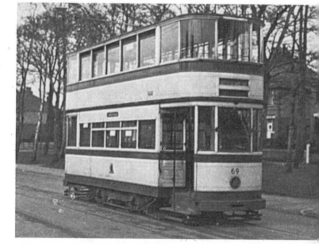

three broad mid-blue bands, and this was gradually extended to the Standard cars. The Roberts cars had a simplified colour scheme of cream with blue bands under the windows of both decks. The elaborate gold lining was continued on both decks of cars still painted in the old style, until as late as 1956.

All cars bore the coat of arms on the lower deck, and a STD (Sheffield Transport Dept) cypher on the upper. Sheffield was one of the last British systems to introduce advertising on the sides of the cars, the first thus appearing in 1954. Even towards the end of operation there was a reluctance to place advertisements on upper deck panels already reserved

for the purpose. The cars were excellently maintained, and kept clean right up to the last year of operation.

Depots were situated at Shoreham Street, Tinsley, near Malin Bridge terminus, Crookes, and at Tenter Street. The latter was a modern building, the 20 tracks on a lower level accommodating 100 cars, while above was a bus garage entered from another street. Tenter Street was the last depot in use. The overhaul works was at Queens Road.

The track was largely welded, and kept in a good state of repair up to the end. The long-wheelbase cars rode very well even in the event of a loose joint, and were not subject to pitching.

An interesting feature was the provision of trolley reversers at all termini. At these points the conductor wire was arranged as a reversing triangle, which was automatic in operation. The car entered the terminus and stood with its trolley in the 'wrong' direction, before reversing slowly over a straight section of track, while the trolley pole followed.

In the early 1950s there were 13 tram services apart from various extra peak workings. The lack of route numbering was most regrettable, but tickets bore an unofficial route designation. There were no through fares across the City centre from one terminus to another: on such a journey one had to pay twice. Sheffield was noted for its low fares. The maximum single fare of 2½d (1p) in 1949 had only risen to 3d by 1951, but by 1960 fares varied between 3½d (1½p) and 8d (3½p).

In the spring of 1951 the City Council confirmed the recommendation of the Transport Committee that

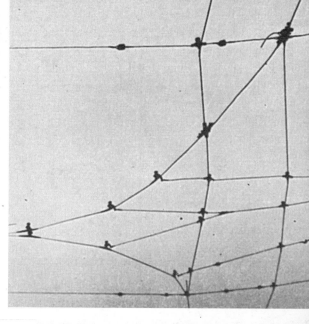

Top left: Abbeydale Road, Beauchief, with Standard car 221 in the experimental but short-lived green livery. (21.9.52)

Bottom left: Works car 349 at Tinsley Depot. (6.6.51)

Top centre: Standard car 145 entering Crookes Depot. (26.9.52)

Top right: Trolley reverser at Eccleshall terminus. (6.6.51)

Bottom right: Straight point-blade in Furnival Street, a connecting line not used for regular traffic. (27.9.52)

the trams be abandoned over a period of 15 years. The ostensible reason was the high cost of replacing older cars by new ones, and the expense of track renewals. It is remarkable that this decision was reached at a time when new cars were still entering service!

Sheffield was one of the few provincial centres where there was strong opposition to tramway closure, and this was indeed fitting, since such a highly developed system was well worth saving. A petition for the retention of tramways was circulated by the Sheffield Tramways Development Association in 1951. However this activity had little effect on the course of events, and in January 1952 the Fulwood to Malin Bridge route became the first to close under the general scheme for conversion of tram routes to bus operation. By March 1960 the tramways were reduced to a north-south configuration, with the Lane Top to Meadowhead, and Tinsley to Beauchief routes still running. Tramway operation ceased with the closing of the latter route on October 8, 1960: Sheffield had been the last industrial city in England with tramways.

Grimsby and Immingham Electric Railway

track, and after about a mile the Grimsby terminus was reached at Corporation Bridge.

The original cars were 54ft 6in long, and thus among the longest ever to run on a British tramway. These cars were originally in brown livery, but together with the Gateshead cars purchased in 1951 for rush hour traffic, were latterly in British Railways' green livery complete with insignia.

An outstanding feature was the heavy traffic to and from Immingham Dock at rush hours, whereas the off-peak traffic was relatively light. In 1956 the line south of Cleveland Bridge was closed, but this new terminus was inconvenient. Operation ceased entirely on July 1, 1961.

The Grimsby & Immingham Electric Railway was one of the few tramways in Britain to be owned by a railway company, being worked successively by the Great Central Railway, London & North Eastern Railway, and British Railways.

The line was built in 1912 to connect the railway-owned docks at Immingham with Grimsby; it was 7¾ miles long and of standard gauge. At Immingham there was a short branch. South thereof the line became single railway track on private right of way, and continued thus in a straight line across the featureless landscape to Pyewipe Depot. South of the depot, at Cleveland Bridge, it became single street

Below: The tramway station at Corporation Bridge, Grimsby, with car 11 of the original batch. (23.9.52)

Right: A convoy of ex-Gateshead cars bound for Grimsby at No 5 Passing Place, about half way along the line. The car turning into the loop is one of the original batch. (23.9.52)

Leeds

From 1909 to 1918 there was a through service between Leeds and Bradford, using cars specially equipped for both gauges! The wheels adjusted from the 4ft 8½in Leeds gauge to the 4ft gauge of Bradford over a tapering section of track at Stanningley. Ten cars were supplied by each City for the service. Through running to the south was not subject to such difficulties; cars of the Yorkshire (West Riding) Electric Tramways Co Ltd ran through from Leeds to Wakefield and Sandal Magna until 1932.

Steady development of the system through the years culminated in the construction of many miles of reserved track. Extensions were opened to connect new housing schemes to the City centre. Thus the Middleton Light Railway was opened in 1925, to connect a new housing scheme on the hills south of the city. The Gipton Estate line was opened in 1937, and after World War II it was intended to extend this route to Seacroft. In 1940 trams reached Belle Isle, were extended 500yds in 1946, and finally reached

In the tramway era Leeds was the main English woollen town, and the most important textile centre in Europe: at one time wool-weaving occupied 70,000 persons and 100 mills. In 1839 there were already horse bus services. Horse tram operation started in 1871, and steam trams were introduced in 1877. By 1883 there were two steam and five horse tram services.

The first electric tramway was opened in 1892 between Sheepscar and Roundhay Park by a private company, and was the first overhead wire tramway in Britain. It was operated with single deck American cars. The first Corporation electric line was opened in 1897 between Kirkstall and Roundhay.

Below: The south side of City Square, with Feltham cars 538 (in foreground) and 532. (18.9.54)

Top right: Loading islands on the east side of City Square, with Horsfield car 187. (12.9.54)

Bottom right: Horsfield car 250 turning from Boar Lane into Briggate. (12.9.54)

Middleton in 1949, thus completing a circular route; this was the last tramway extension.

At its maximum extent the system consisted of 68 route miles. However considerable portions had been closed before World War II, notably the Guiseley route beyond Kirkstall Abbey, as well as the Rodney and Pudsey branches off the Stanningley route. In 1947 some sections which involved much single and loop, including Cardigan Road and Lower Wortley, were closed. There then followed some five years of stability. In 1952 there were 394 cars operating over 47 miles of route, of which 10½ miles were reserved track.

In the City centre there was no possibility of alternative routeings, since Boar Lane was the only connection between east and west. The nerve centre was the imposing City Square, surrounded by important buildings, and with the City Station on the south side. There was ample room for pedestrians, besides the statues, fountains and seats. All stops there were on loading islands. Boar Lane, a none too wide thoroughfare, had no stops. In Briggate, at the junction with Boar Lane, the maximum use was made of the rather cramped layout by the arrangement of two central loading islands with passenger shelters and queueing arrangements. At the Corn Exchange there was a turning circle for short workings, as well as a loop for those from the eastern districts.

Beyond City Square, the routes to the western termini of New Inn, Whingate, Stanningley and Kirkstall Abbey passed the 'dark satanic mills' of industrial development. The main overhaul works was situated on the latter route. The New Inn and Whingate routes crossed the Leeds and Liverpool Canal, then still open for commercial traffic, with one or two steam barges at work. Next an area of drab back-to-back working class houses of typical north

Above: Wellington Street near Central station, with a Feltham car. (12.9.54)

Top right: Radial-axle car 444 at Kirkstall Abbey terminus. (4.6.51)

Centre right: New Inn terminus, Tong Road, with Feltham car 529. The housing was typical of the older working class areas of the city. (12.9.54)

Bottom right: Gipton Estate terminus, with radial-truck car 52. (8.6.51)

country type was traversed. Some of the side streets gave the impression of never having any traffic, for it was common to find grass growing in the road. Latterly the Stanningley route terminated at Half Mile Lane.

The south and south-west of the City was of similar character, especially the Hunslet route, which was most depressing. At right angles to Elland Road terminus was a spur on Low Fields Road for specials to the Leeds United football ground. On Saturday afternoons in the season it was a fine sight to see long lines of cars waiting to carry the supporters home, and this spectacle could also be glimpsed from trains approaching the City Station.

The pride of the system was the Middleton route. This was street track as far as Moor Road, Hunslet, and from that point on was known as the Middleton Light Railway, running on its own tracks through the idyllic Middleton Woods. When the circle was completed, route 12 ran anti-clockwise, and route 26 in the opposite direction. The City boarding point for Middleton cars was well hidden away in Swinegate, in

a most unprepossessing area beneath the railway viaduct leading to City Station. Cars for Middleton and Belle Isle ran inward via Bridge End and outward via Neville Street.

Apart from the first 1¼ miles from Corn Exchange through old badly-bombed areas, the York Road routes to the east were a model of what a modern tramway layout should be. At the junction of York Street and York Road, the Compton Road street line branched to the left. At Torre Road Depot, opened in 1937, the line went on to reservation. Five-eighths of a mile beyond, the Gipton Estate route diverged to the left. This was notable for the cutting to ease the gradient to the terminus, beyond which were still green fields in the early 1950s. Just beyond the Templenewsam route branched off to the right. This portion had a 30-minute service on weekdays, but only a 50-minute service on Sundays; however Halton cars went almost to the entrance of Templenewsam Park, the largest public open space in the Leeds area, consisting partly of attractive woodlands, the last part of the private right of way actually passing through the Park. The main line to Crossgates continued straight on, skirting open country for half a mile before reaching the modern suburb at the terminus, near which there was a section of street track.

The routes to the northern suburbs traversed more pleasant older built-up areas with some villa development, but there was little reserved track. Proceeding north from City Square, the Lawnswood route passed for a short distance through the business area and served the modern University. Shortly afterwards Woodhouse Moor was crossed, this section being a kind of semi-reservation, with islands between the tracks. At Headingley the route passed close to the cricket ground, and then the Depot was seen on the right. Further on was a more modern development

Above: University, Woodhouse Lane, with Horsfield car. (17.9.54)

Centre right: Headingley, St Michael's Lane, with Chamberlain car 130. (17.9.54)

Bottom right: Chamberlain car 71 standing at West Park, Ring Road, where there was an extra track for short-working cars. (16.9.54)

of large Victorian houses culminating in a pleasant area of trees at West Park, a short-working point, before the terminus was reached along three-quarters of a mile of reserved track.

The other north side routes passed through the City's main shopping area. At Meanwood Road the Meanwood route branched off to the west, and immediately after was the junction where the Chapeltown and Roundhay loop joined. The loop served a superior residential area, with correspondingly more pleasant surroundings. There was an attractive stretch of reserved track about a mile in length through Roundhay Park.

Leeds was interesting to the tramway student from the rolling stock point of view. For example in 1951 there were at least ten different types of car to be seen, including three types of second hand cars.

Above: Princes Avenue, Roundhay Park, with Chamberlain car 96. The sleepers are exposed for track renewal. (25.9.52)

Right: Chamberlain car 56 at Lawnswood terminus in dark red livery. (16.9.54)

The oldest cars still running in the early 1950s were the Chamberlain type, which dated from the 1920s. These vehicles were originally mounted on radial trucks, an attempt to emulate the riding qualities of a bogie car. The riding of these cars was so bad that it was decided about 1945 to re-truck them with rigid trucks. By 1948 half the cars had been so converted. A big drawback of these cars (as well as of the Horsfield type) was that the upper deck end windows were totally occupied by the route and number indicators, a feature which showed a lamentable lack of imagination on the part of the designers.

The mainstay of the fleet until the arrival of the Feltham cars was the Horsfield type. These cars dated from about 1930, and had flush-panelled sides, a seat for the driver, platform doors, and air-brakes. The appearance was conventional but neat.

The first Middleton bogie appeared in 1933, and the production batch of 16 followed in 1935. The

Above: Horsfield car in dark blue livery, at Lawnswood terminus. (4.6.51)

Right: Horsfield car 232 in dark blue livery, at Meanwood terminus. (8.6.51)

prototype was 36ft long, but the rest were 6in shorter. The cars had the unusual feature of a staircase next to the entrance, and seated 70. Normally they were confined to the Middleton line, but occasionally ran on the Moortown, Roundhay and Lawnswood routes; latterly they were also seen on the York Road services. The last was withdrawn in 1957, after which the Middleton line was worked by Horsfield and Feltham cars.

The two four-wheel streamlined cars built by Leeds before World War II were always known as 'Lance-Corporals', because of the V-paintwork at the ends. The cars were attractive and comfortable; one can only regret that more of this type were not built.

Car 275 was a utility four-wheeler built in World War II, of neat and practical design. Soon after the war, it was intended to purchase 50 new cars, but no manufacturer was able to deliver them: it must be remembered that at this time the shortage of materials meant that very few buses could be built. The decision to build new cars in the workshops was stillborn. The

first new post-war car was 276, very similar to 275. It appeared in September 1948 in light blue livery, and had straight staircases. It could always be distinguished from 275 by the rounded ends.

Two fine new cars, 601 and 602, entered service in June 1953. The bodies were identical and of composite construction, and were by Charles H. Roe Ltd. The cars were 41ft 5in long, weighed about 17tons, and had room for 34 seated and 36 standing passengers. Car 601 had EMB trucks with rubber-insert wheels and conventional equipment, while 602 was the first British all-electric car, having PCC-type trucks and equipment, the bogies being of the inside-frame type. Both cars were capable of about 50mph, and were finished in an extravagant livery of purple lined with gold and cream, to mark the Coronation of Queen Elizabeth II. The cars were intended to be the forerunners of a new fleet.

The ex-Sunderland single decker, purchased in 1944 (!), appeared about the same time, as car 600,

Left: Middleton bogie 265 in light blue livery at Middleton. (8.6.51)

Below: Lance Corporal car 274 in light blue livery at Headingley. (4.6.51)

after having been completely reconstructed over a period of years. It was a veritable amalgam of secondhand components from many sources, even including London Underground coaches!

Leeds was notable among the larger systems in relying to a large extent on secondhand cars during the last decade of operation. Just before World War II, three HR/2 cars had been purchased from London, and received the numbers 277-279. They always ran from Chapeltown Depot and were generally noted for their lively performance, but apparently drivers tried to make service stops on 279 using the hand brake only, in which event no great speed was possible.

As a matter of policy it was decided after World War II to purchase any suitable secondhand cars. A number of cars made redundant by abandonments were bought from Hull, and a last batch of ten was bought on the closure of that system in 1946. In 1948 50 ex-Hull cars were running in Leeds; they had replaced the last of the open-balcony Leeds cars.

In 1949 seven Pilcher cars were bought from Manchester, as well as 11 Domed-Roof cars from Southampton, and put into service. Both those systems closed in 1949. Some cars bought from Southampton were in poor condition, and did not enter service. Both types were much inferior to the Horsfield and ex-London cars, and had only a short lease of life in Leeds.

Feltham car 2099 from London ran experimentally in Leeds from October 1949 to August 1950 (still with its London number), before being renumbered 501. The tests were successful, so that 89 more cars were purchased at £500 each, a bargain when one considers that new cars then cost at least twenty times that figure! The rest of the cars were delivered between August 1950 and October 1951. The bodies of the

Above: Wartime utility car 275 in light blue livery at Corn Exchange. (4.6.51)

Top right: Coronation car 601 in purple livery at Hunslet terminus. (16.9.54)

Centre right: Ex-Sunderland car 600 in dark red livery at Hunslet terminus. (16.9.54)

Bottom right: Ex-London HR/2 car 277 in dark red livery at Headingley Depot. (25.9.52)

Felthams were found to be in good condition. They were attached to Torre Road Depot, and rode well on the reserved track, but were underpowered for Leeds gradients. The Felthams were latterly the most numerous type, and were in service to the end.

The luxury London car 1 was transferred to Leeds in April 1951 after closure of the Croydon routes, becoming Leeds 301; early in 1952 it was in service from Chapeltown Depot. Judging from the worn condition of this car after withdrawal in Leeds, it saw more service in eight years in Leeds than in the previous 19 in London!

The original Leeds livery was dark blue and cream, but this was superseded between about 1948 and 1953 by a light blue and cream colour scheme. It is possible that the Leeds-built car 276 was the first to appear so painted, and ex-London 279 the last. In 1951 dark red and cream were adopted as the standard colours, after a number of experimental colour schemes had been tried on the Felthams.

Depots were situated in the early 1950s at Chapeltown, Torre Road, Swinegate and Headingley, the works being at Kirkstall Road. The permanent

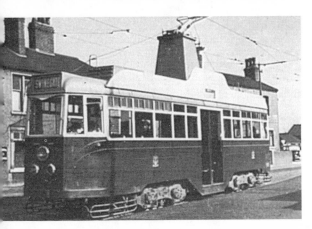

way yard was opposite Swinegate Depot. Cars were scrapped in a yard near Elland Road terminus.

The street track was severely corrugated even as early as 1948. The reserved track was laid originally on a concrete foundation, and perhaps for that reason the four-wheelers did not ride at all well on it. Span wires were used on the reserved track sections, but the Middleton Light Railway and Roundhay Park had centre poles.

Due to the restricted layout in the City centre, there were few through services. Whingate — Crossgates and New Inn — Halton were exceptions. A peculiarity of the numbering scheme was that each suburban terminus was allotted a separate number. This meant that the through working bore a different number in each direction, ie Halton — New Inn 16, but New Inn — Halton 20. Services were frequent, with about ten-minute intervals. The maximum fare in 1948 was 3d (1p). The changeover to Ultimate tickets was started in 1949.

As a result of a change in local government, when the Labour group won control of the City Council, there was a snap decision to abandon the tramways. It is true that the trams were running at a loss, but revenue covered most of the operating costs, which were only marginally above those of the buses. Under this pretext the fate of the trams was sealed at the same time as the railcars entered service: the parallel with Sheffield and Glasgow will be noted, though in Leeds the waste of new assets was not so great. Later in 1953 the Half Mile Lane route became the first to close, buses being used for this and later replacements.

Up to the end of 1956, all the northern and western routes had been abandoned, together with Compton Road and Gipton in the east, and Beeston in the south-west. This left the Middleton and York Road routes,

Above: Ex-Manchester Pilcher car 283 in light blue livery at Hunslet terminus. (9.6.51)

Right: Ex-Southampton car 291 in Street Lane, Moortown. (4.6.51)

which had a high proportion of reserved track, as well as Elland Road, Dewsbury Road and Hunslet. The Middleton Light Railway closed in March 1959.

The last routes in operation, those from Corn Exchange to Crossgates and Templenewsam, were worked by Horsfield and Feltham cars running from Torre Road Depot, and finally closed on November 7, 1959.

Right: Ex-London Feltham car 503 in experimental livery of dark red at Halton. (4.6.51)

Below: Car body in Shirley Depot Yard, Southampton, awaiting transport to Leeds. (6.6.49)

Bottom: Stores car 4A towing a wagon loaded with rails in Swinegate, followed by Chamberlain car 123. (16.9.54)

Blackburn

One of the most important textile centres in Britain, Blackburn at one time had steam trams, and the first electric cars ran on the Preston Road route in 1899. From 1900 a joint service of Blackburn and Darwen cars ran between the two towns. Blackburn cars ran through to Accrington from 1907, and ten years later this became a joint service, ceasing with the closure of the Accrington portion in 1932.

At its maximum the system amounted to about 15 miles of route on 4ft gauge. The town centre layout was complex, and involved one way working for all routes. Elsewhere there was much interlaced track, and in one case at least the interlaced lines were connected by a crossover!

At one time there were 61 bogie cars, 13 of which were single deckers. Eight of the double deckers had maximum traction trucks, and the rest equal-wheel trucks, all the former and eight of the latter never receiving top covers; all these cars were still in stock in World War II. A peculiarity of the double deckers was the level lower deck floor, without the usual step up from the platform, but this in turn meant that there was an extra step up to the platform from street level. The platform was closed off to the public by an obsolete trellis gate. The forbidding, angular design tended to date the vehicles more than might have otherwise been the case, but the fact remains that the equal-wheel cars were renowned for their smooth and steady running. The livery was olive green and cream, but the paintwork was very neglected during the last few years of operation.

On September 20, 1941 a Darwen car overturned in Blackburn, and on March 24, 1942 there was a head-on collision between two tramcars in Bolton Road, on the Darwen route. Darwen had intended to close its section of the through route to Blackburn in 1940, but was obliged to keep it running because of wartime shortages. However the service came to an end with the closure of this last part of the Darwen tramways in 1946.

Most of the Blackburn system survived World War II, but by 1949 only the Church and Darwen Boundary routes were still running. The inner section of the Church route as far as Intack was the last to survive, and closed on September 3, 1949: the nine-road Intack Depot had latterly become a scrap yard for the trams.

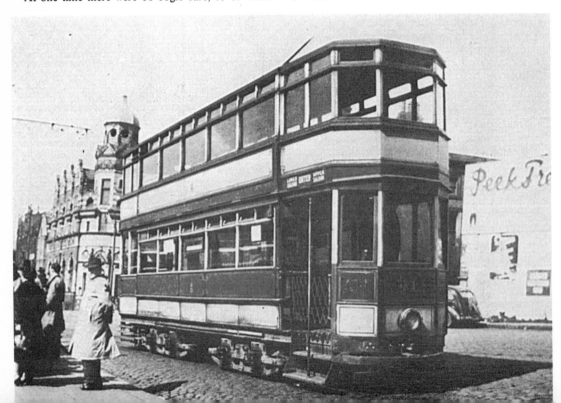

Left: Car 41 bound for Intack on a siding at the railway station. (18.4.49)

Above: Cars 41 and 64 at Darwen Boundary. (18.4.49)

Right: Car 53 in partially dismantled state at Intack Depot. (18.4.49)

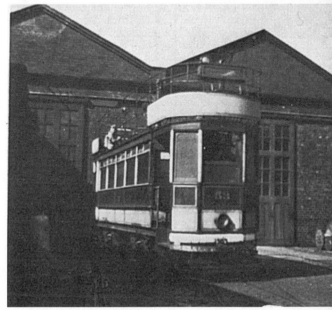

Blackpool

The Blackpool and Fleetwood Tramroad, eight miles long, was opened in 1898 by a company of that name between North Station and Fleetwood, reaching the sea front at Gynn Square. Fleetwood did not take up its option to buy its section, and the line was acquired by Blackpool in 1920, so that the Corporation operated 20½ miles of standard gauge route. Through cars ran from Lytham St Annes to Gynn Square, Blackpool between 1922 and 1937.

The Central Drive and Layton routes were closed in 1933, but this coincided with the introduction of new single deck railcoaches, which were closely followed by other modern types. By 1939 the Promenade route was worked entirely by modern cars. Turning circles were opened at Pleasure Beach, Starr Gate and Little Bispham in the late 1930s; these were rare on British tramways, and contributed greatly to the rapid turnround of traffic. Additional tracks were installed at various points along the coastal route, to enable reversing cars to be overtaken.

The operating cost per car mile in 1949 was among the lowest of any British tramway at 20.2d (8p), a tribute to the value of modernisation. Early in 1952

Not only has Blackpool the oldest electric tramway system in the world still running, but the only one remaining in England. The outstanding feature is the holiday traffic, whereby an intensive service is required for a brief season. Conduit electric cars operated by the Blackpool Electric Tramways Co Ltd started running in 1884. The line was taken over by the Corporation in 1892, extended in 1895 and 1897, and converted to overhead operation in 1899. There were originally ten conduit cars, and the Corporation added four more. The Marton and Layton routes were opened in 1901 and 1903 respectively, on the overhead system.

Right: Promenade and Tower at Talbot Square, with Railcoaches and Coronation car. (15.6.56)

Below: The Talbot Square terminus of the route to Marton, with Railcoach 11 and Standard car 152. (11.5.49)

Above: The three-track layout at Cabin, with car 705. (14.9 74)

Centre right: Car 170 passing the Miners' Home, Bispham, on its way to North station, Blackpool. (15.6.56)

Bottom right: Queen's Parade, Bispham, with car 710. (14.9.74)

Far right, top: Car 718 on the turning circle at Little Bispham. (13.9.74)

there were 18 miles of route, with about 200 cars. The routes then worked were Starr Gate — Fleetwood, North Station — Fleetwood, Squires Gate — Bispham, and Talbot Square — Royal Oak (in summer extended to South Pier). The system stayed intact until 1961, when the Squires Gate route closed. The Marton route closed in 1962, and with it Marton Depot; in the winter of 1961-62 the Marton route had had a four-minute service.

The closure of the Dickson Road line to North Station in 1963 reduced the tramways to the coastal line only, a distance of 11 miles, with a journey time of 56 minutes. Bispham Depot was closed at the same time, but later temporarily reopened.

In the winter of 1961-62 the coastal line had a 12-minute service, but in the winter of 1963-64 trams ran between Cleveleys and Fleetwood only, the section southwards to Starr Gate being replaced by buses, but through cars were restored in the following winter. The number of passengers has declined from some 40 millions in the mid-1950s to about 11 millions, this

being accounted for only in part by the closure of routes.

The coastal route starts in the south at Starr Gate, where there is a turning circle. Just north thereof, the line swings on to the Promenade, the tracks being on the seaward side of the carriageway, level with but not separated from the pedestrian way. This arrangement continues as far as Talbot Square in the centre of the town. The lack of pedestrian crossings on the Promenade makes it difficult to reach the trams in the busy season.

One mile beyond Starr Gate, a large garish amusement area is passed. North of South Pier, at Manchester Square, the line to Rigby Road Depot branches inland. The line also connects with the works and Blundell Street store. Beyond Central Pier, the line reaches the Tower, the limit of the low-lying area. South thereof, the tracks are frequently affected by blown sand and high tides, while salt spray and sand have serious effects on car paintwork. At Talbot Square, the shopping area is but a few minutes walk away. Immediately beyond, the line is laid in the road for 200yd, after which it runs well above sea level.

The trams run on a fenced-in reservation as far as the outskirts of Fleetwood. Thornton Gate is the main centre between Blackpool and Fleetwood, and the line passes inland, and on to the landward side of the coastal road. At Rossall the development thinned to become semi-rural, but this picturesque part of the route has recently been built up.

The tramway through Fleetwood is street track, this being (apart from the 200yd at Blackpool) the sole remaining street tramway in Britain. The ride through Fleetwood is unremarkable, but car parking is allowed on both sides of the road, so that it is not possible for traffic to overtake the trams. The line describes a large loop, one-way running commencing at the lighthouse, and the terminus is at the Ferry.

The first cars built for the overhead system were the Dreadnoughts, which had double staircases at each end. In 1901-03 fifteen four-wheel open top and twelve bogie open top cars were built, as well as eight more Dreadnoughts. They were followed in 1911-12 by seven top covered cars, as well as by 24 toastracks, built 1911-14.

Thirty-three Standard cars were built in 1923-27, and the 1901-03 cars were rebuilt to this design. The last Standard was withdrawn in 1966. A final batch of six toastracks was built in 1927.

The last conventional type cars entered service in 1928; they were single deckers 167-176, built for the Fleetwood route. They were finally withdrawn in 1960.

A new type of single deck centre-entrance car was built in 1933, with 48 seats, a separate cab for the driver, and a length of nearly 41ft. Altogether 65 such cars were built in 1933-37. They were followed in 1939 by a further 12, but that batch had wooden seats, and savings were made on equipment, since they were intended only for seasonal use. The cars were improved in 1942, and further modernised about 1948-50, making them comparable with the earlier Railcoaches, as the modern single deckers were known, being fitted with florescent lights and Vambac control equipment. They were used on the Marton route, which was completely relaid about that time, the old track being badly worn and extensively corrugated.

Twelve modern open single deckers were built in 1934. In that year also 13 modern open top 94-seat double deckers appeared, these cars being top-covered in 1941. Fourteen totally enclosed double deckers of luxurious appointment were built in 1935, and entered service on the Squires Gate route. The cars ran to Fleetwood for the first time in 1958, after check rails had been inserted on the reserved track.

Railcoaches 303 and 208 were experimentally fitted with PCC-type bogies and Vambac multi-notch equipment in 1946, and trials lasted for several years. The cars were painted with cream lower panels to distinguish them from the others. In the early 1950s a number of cars were fitted with resilient wheels and Vambac equipment.

These experiments led to the introduction of the Coronation type in 1952. Twenty-five were built; they were 50ft long, 8ft wide and had four 45hp motors, as well as resilient wheels and Vambac equipment.

In 1958 a motor and trailer set rebuilt from 1935 Railcoaches was introduced. This led to the purchase of ten trailers, delivered in 1960-61; railcoaches 272-281 were rebuilt to resemble them. The combinations were known as Twin-Sets, and were normally permanently coupled.

Top right: Little Bispham, with car 705. (14.9.74)

Centre right: Standard cars 145 (left) and 42 at Talbot Square terminus. (12.5.49)

Below: Car 167 at Fleetwood terminus. (12.5.49)

There were still 180 cars in 1961, but with route closures and reduction in carryings this had fallen to 122 by 1964, the average age of all cars being about 23 years, while nearly three-quarters of the fleet was of pre-1939 origin. In the following five years the fleet was further reduced by 18 cars, and the first Coronation was broken up for spare parts in 1968, until in 1974 only four remained!

Five one-man cars with new bodies, but old trucks and equipment, entered service in 1972; there are now eight of these cars running. They are fast, but delayed by the need of the driver to collect fares. Several of the cars built in the 1930s have been rebuilt or refurbished. The entire fleet was renumbered in 1968.

The former red and cream livery was changed to green and cream in 1933. There have been several versions of this, so that at first cars had cream lower panels, then green, while in recent years there has been a reversion to cream. One-man cars are orange with a red roof. Advertisements were not carried until 1959, and of recent years the box-like constructions carried by some cars for advertising purposes greatly detracted from the appearance of the vehicles.

Apart from depots already mentioned, Rigby Road is now the main running shed, having been opened in 1935. Blundell Street Depot was then closed, and remained a store until 1956, when it became a bus

Top right: Railcoach 216 at Squires Gate terminus. (15.6.56)

Centre right: Car 723 at Bispham after rebuilding. (14.9.74)

Below: Car 208, fitted with resilient wheels and Vambac equipment, at Rigby Road Depot. (17.4.49)

garage, but returned to use as a tram store in 1963, as a result of the closure of Marton Depot.

The permanent way sidings are situated at Thornton Gate. There was formerly a permanent way depot at Copse Road, Fleetwood. Of recent years much work has been done on welding the track, and not before time, for the reserved tracks were noted to be considerably the worse for wear in 1968. The first German NP 4 (Normal Profile) rail was delivered in 1966, and cost five times as much as rail purchased 30 years earlier. Tram rail is no longer rolled in Britain. Blackpool is the only British tramway system to have provided for the operation of cars wider than 7ft 3in. This was done by widening the clearance between the tracks on the coastal line as relaying became due. In September 1974 the street track sections were noted to be the best, with very good paving; reserved track was in fair condition. No rail corrugation was encountered, nor were any cars heard with flatted wheels, despite the inclement weather.

A special feature in the autumn is the operation of tours of the illuminations, and of illuminated and decorated cars. In summer students and part-time conductors are employed.

By 1966 the trams were running at a loss, and traffic had dropped by half since 1961. The trams carried only one-quarter of the local traffic, since there is an extensive bus network, including the replacement for former tram routes. Great savings have been made in operation, and the introduction of one-man cars gives substance to the hope that trams may have a future in Blackpool.

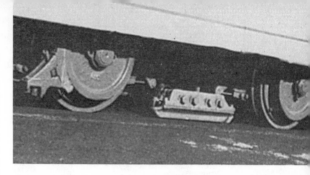

Top left: Truck of car 208. (17.4.49)

Centre left: Car 208 on the Promenade. (12.5.49)

Bottom left: One-man car 5 at Bispham. (14.9.74)

Right: Engineering car 753, converted from a Standard, at Little Bispham turning circle. (14.9.74)

Below: Bispham Depot, with 1928 cars on the right. (15.6.56)

Manx Electric Railway

The Manx Electric Railway is one of the few true interurbans ever to have existed in the British Isles, and one of the two remaining electric tramways. Moreover it traverses a holiday area of great natural beauty, and is undoubtedly the most scenic tramway to have been built in Britain.

The 3ft gauge line was opened between Douglas and Groudle Glen in 1893 as a single track (but was soon doubled), and was extended in 1894 to Laxey, in 1895 to Ballure, and finally to Ramsey in 1899. Originally bow collectors were used, but by 1898 they had been replaced by trolley poles.

Much of the traffic on the line came and still comes from tourists, but until the 1920s stone, cattle and goods traffic was important. To handle this there were at one time more than a dozen wagons, as well as some special stone carriers and an electric locomotive. At Dhoon Glen there was a spur to a stone quarry. A number of the smaller vans still exist.

The 18-mile long route is entirely double track and does not run in the public road at any point, but there are one or two road crossings where the trams secure right of way by setting traffic lights to red for motor traffic. The Douglas to Laxey section generally runs close to public roads, whereas the remainder to Ramsey has a high proportion of private right of way away from roads.

The coast is followed for more than a mile and a half at the Douglas end, and also on each side of Laxey, but the track is high above the sea. Apart from at Laxey, where the line passes over a viaduct and connects with the 3ft 6in gauge Snaefell Mountain Railway, the route lies through unspoilt country. The Snaefell Mountain Railway is an overhead electric line

Below: Derby Castle terminus Douglas, with Corporation horse car, Manx Electric car 6 (in background), and Corporation wartime Daimler bus 52. (12.6.56)

Top right: Early morning car with goods van containing mail at Derby Castle, Douglas. (9.6.56)

Centre right: View near Howstrake, with car 22. (12.6.56)

Bottom right: Douglas-bound train at Laxey Bay. (12.6.56)

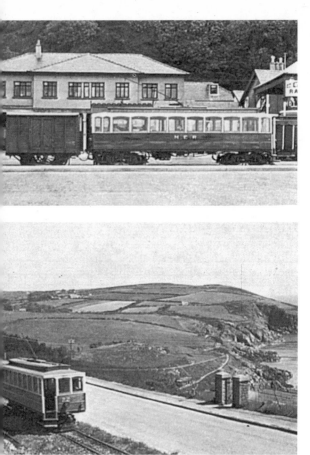

equipped with a Fell centre rack rail, and ascends the bare mountainside to a height of just over 2,000ft.

The Manx Electric approach to Laxey is particularly fine, with an enchanting view of Laxey Bay before traversing a wooded area into the town. Beyond the line climbs steadily to Bulgham Bay, where the highest point of nearly 600ft above sea level is reached, and here there is a sheer drop to the sea. Further on there are more views of the sea, and the peninsula between there and Ramsey is dominated by North Barrule, at 1,860ft the second highest peak on the island. The line passes over a viaduct at Ballure just before entering Walpole Road, the only portion laid with grooved rail.

There are 24 motors and 24 trailers, the average age of all cars being about 70 years! The motors consist of two unvestibuled cars, built in 1893; eight vestibuled saloons, four of which were built in 1894 and four in 1899; and fourteen open cars built between 1898 and 1906. The four 1899 saloons 19-22 are used in winter. All motor cars are fitted with four motors, mainly of at least 25hp each.

Twenty-one of the trailers are open cars, six dating from 1893 and two from 1894. The rest were built between 1896 and 1906, except for three dating from 1930. The open trailers have roller shutters which can be let down over the sides. The saloons were built in 1895 and 1904.

The livery was red, brown and white, but 14 cars were repainted in green and white in 1958. However there was soon a return to the old colour scheme.

The depot and works is at the Douglas terminus. Other sheds are situated at Laxey and Ramsey. A fire

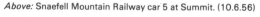

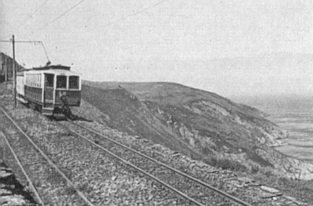

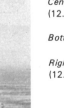

Above: Snaefell Mountain Railway car 5 at Summit. (10.6.56)

Centre left: Bulgham Bay looking north, with car 19 and trailer. (12.6.56)

Bottom left: Walpole Road, Ramsey, with car 19. (10.6.56)

Right: Car 19 and trailer passing Maughold Head near Ramsey. (12.6.56)

at Laxey Depot in 1930 destroyed four motors and seven open trailers.

The track is flat bottomed rail laid on wooden sleepers. In spite of the hilly nature of the route, the maximum gradient is only 1:24, and there are no sharp curves. The overhead is of centre-pole construction throughout.

The winter of 1951-52 was the first without a Sunday service. The reason was a drop in traffic; on weekdays there were some ten journeys each way between Douglas and Ramsey. In the mid-1950s there were 19 through cars to Ramsey on weekdays and 12 on Sundays, but the Douglas to Laxey section had a 15-minute service with short workings.

In 1957 the Manx Electric was taken over from the Company by the Manx Government, and this saved it from closure. Under the new ownership, substantial improvements were made to the track. Between 1957 and 1962 about half the track and sleepers between Douglas and Laxey were renewed, and track improvement has continued in recent years.

93

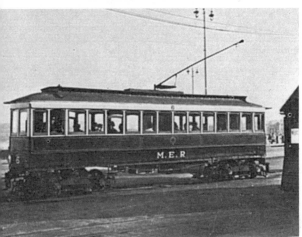

In the financial year 1965-66, 434,000 passengers were carried. A Transport Commission set up by the Manx Government reported in 1966 that the Laxey to Ramsey section should be closed because it was uneconomic.

The collapse of the retaining wall below the line at Bulgham in January 1967 cut through services, and cars had to terminate at each side until July. At first there were fears that this might furnish an excuse to close the Laxey to Ramsey portion, but these were quickly dispelled by repair work.

The summer service in 1969 was roughly hourly, cars usually running with trailers at this time of year. The return fare between Douglas and Ramsey was 7/9d (39p) in 1969, but reduced fare tickets including the Snaefell Mountain Railway were also issued in summer.

In winter two motors suffice to maintain the service. It remains to be seen how long the line can exist without any new rolling stock, even if this consists of only two or three cars for the winter. Up to now the Manx Electric has managed to survive largely on tourist traffic in a limited season, but this can hardly be a healthy basis for continuance. It will be tragic if the renewed threat to close the Laxey to Ramsey section, by far the most scenic, is implemented.

Far left: Car 9, built in 1894, at Derby Castle, Douglas terminus. (12.6.56)

Top left: Car 21 and vans at Ramsey terminus. (10.6.56)

Centre left: Car 6, built in 1894, at Derby Castle, Douglas terminus. (9.6.56)

Below: Car 19, built in 1899, at Derby Castle, Douglas terminus. (10.6.56)

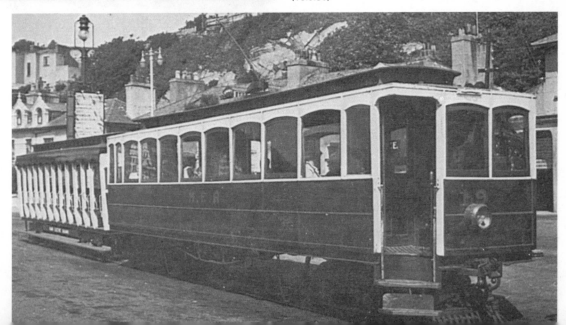

Belfast

Although later converted to standard gauge, the first horse car line of 1872 was of 5ft 3in gauge. Belfast was one of the last large cities in the United Kingdom to adopt electric tramways, the system being opened virtually complete in 1905, with 170 cars. Some horse cars were converted to electric traction; there were eventually 50 of these in open top and covered top state, the last being withdrawn in 1948. While this is remarkable proof of the quality of construction of horse cars, retention of such ancient vehicles in traffic conditions for which they were not designed helped to give the tram a bad name.

The electric line from Cavehill to Glengormley was owned by a private company until 1911, and had the only single track on the system. Extensions were made to the tramways in 1908 and 1912, and then not until the 1920s, the last new tramway being opened in 1925.

The maximum number of cars in use at any one time was about 380.

Cars worked into the railway stations at York Road and Queens Quay. The Queens Road route, serving the shipyards, was in the peak hour one of the busiest sections of tramway in the United Kingdom. Latterly the trams were blamed for congestion on Queens Bridge.

Belfast cars were always of the four-wheel type. Some 230-odd Standard cars were built from 1905 on, with 58 seats, these and the ex-horse cars all being open top. Many of the cars were totally enclosed from 1929 on. The eight cars inherited from the Cavehill and Whitewell line were of similar design.

In 1919 the Moffett cars were introduced, of which 50 were built. They seated 68, originally had a forward exit, and were totally enclosed. The Chamberlain cars appeared in 1930. Fifty were built, and at 33ft they were the longest Belfast cars, having 66 seats.

The McCreary cars were a modern 1935 design, and some were built at Sandy Row Works. There were 64 seats and a cab for the driver, as well as folding platform doors. The cars were 32ft long, and 50 were built.

Right: Chamberlain car 357 climbing to Ligoniel terminus. (17.6.53)

Below: McCreary car 440 at Ligoniel terminus. (17.6.53)

The original livery was red and cream with gold lining, but in 1929 a new colour scheme of blue and cream was adopted. The last red cars did not disappear until about 1950.

Depots were at one time situated at Ardoyne, Mount Pottinger, Shore Road, Falls Road, Knock Road, Salisbury Avenue and Sandy Row (also works).

The first route to close was that to Falls Road, in 1938. Even during the war years, closures took place on the east side of the system! Early in 1950 there were still 200 cars in use, all of which had upholstered seats, serving 16 routes on the west side of the City. Twenty open balcony cars were in use in the peak for the Queens Road shipyard traffic, this being the only remaining regular route in east Belfast, though extra cars worked to Queens Quay Station, and there were depot workings to Mount Pottinger. A peculiarity was the provision of a peak hours only service on routes from which regular cars had been withdrawn. This was not unknown elsewhere (ie the Millbrook route in Southampton), but perhaps nowhere else was it practised to the same extent.

There were still 20 miles of the maximum 51½ miles of route in use at the beginning of 1952. The following routes were still open: York Road Station, Ligoniel,

Above: Mount Pottinger Depot during the evening rush hour, with McCreary car 394 leaving. This shed had a capacity of nearly 100 cars. (15.6.53)

Top right: Disabled McCreary car being fitted with a new trolleyhead at Castle Junction in the City centre. (15.6.53)

Bottom right: McCreary car 418 leaving Queens Quay station. (20.6.53)

Ballygomartin, Springfield Road, Balmoral and Queens Road. Depots were at Ardoyne, Sandy Row and Mount Pottinger, while Shore Road Depot was used as a store.

Up to and including World War II, tramways had been replaced by trolleybuses, but later buses were used. The last trams ran on February 27 1954.

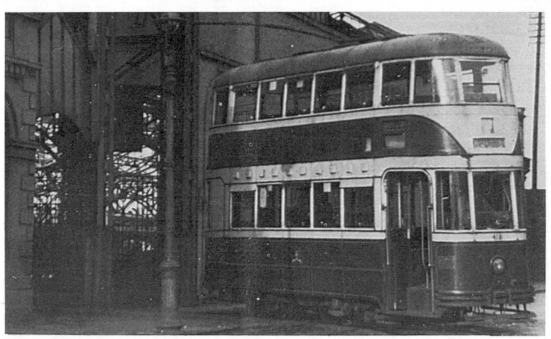

Glasgow

The most notable feature of Glasgow in the tramway era was the shipbuilding industry. In the mid-1950s one third of all British tonnage was still launched on the Clyde, the nearest competitor achieving only half this figure.

The first horse trams started running in Glasgow in 1872. Glasgow bedame in 1898 one of the first cities to operate electric trams, when the Mitchell Street to Springburn route was opened. Eventually the system included those of Paisley and Airdrie, the latter being connected to the Glasgow tramways by a reserved track from Baillieston to Langloan, opened in 1923. The network was the second largest in Britain after London.

The City boundary was last extended in 1912, this resulted in nearly half the route mileage being outside Glasgow. In 1952 there were 133 miles of 4ft 7¾ in gauge route, this gauge having been adopted to permit the use of the tracks by normal railway vehicles running on their flanges. After World War II two shipyards in Govan still worked goods tains hauled by electric locomotives over the tramways.

The grid-iron layout in the central area had an unfortunate effect on tramway operation, in that numerous right-angle turns were necessary. The City centre had very heavy motor traffic, and latterly the trams were blamed for the congestion. This was partly correct, for there passengers boarded and alighted mainly in the roadway.

For its size the system had remarkably little reserved track, but even then operation on such sections was very slow. South of the Clyde reservations existed only at Mosspark Boulevard, and between Thornliebank and Barrhead, the approach to the latter being along country lanes. At Paisley Road Toll there was a curious but effective arrangement, whereby routes formerly crossing at a very acute angle were separated from each other.

Below: George Square, City Chambers, with a Coronation car. (18.6.57)

Top right: Trongate, Tron Church, with ex-Liverpool car. (18.6.57)
Centre right: Argyle Street, Central station, with Standard car 298. (16.6.57)

Bottom right: Cunarder car 1367 at University. (30.7.52)

The south-eastern routes and those serving the inner part of the southern area traversed run down districts. The sout-western lines provided an attractive contrast, with modern housing and wooded surroundings.

The 600yd Thornliebank-Carnwadrie street tramway extension was opened in February 1949, and concurrently tram routes 2 and 19 were replaced by buses, the former pending conversion to trolleybuses. At the same time, work started on what was to be the last tramway extension, that of the Great Western Road reserved track from Knightswood to Blairdardie.

At Dalmuir West the trams passed over the Forth & Clyde Canal by an opening swing bridge, and at Maryhill the Canal actually crossed the tramway on an aqueduct. The long Milngavie route served superior housing areas, while modern housing was to be found at the end of the Riddrie route.

A remarkable feature was the roadside reservation between Baillieston and Langloan. This two mile long line was of true interurban nature, and traversed an area not the built up. Coronation cars ran on this route, but regrettably to extremely slack schedules no doubt due to older cars sharing the service.

Altogether 1,300 cars were built at Coplawhill Works, and only 50 of the fleet (the Kilmarnock bogies) were not built there. The proportion of modern cars was however low, for in 1954 only 282 of the 1,067 were of modern design.

The Standard cars formed the basis of the fleet. These could be divided broadly into two types, the round dash and hexagonal dash cars. The vehicles had

Above: Clarkston terminus, with two types of Standard car, of which 157 is in the foreground. (14.9.50)

Top right: The beginning of the reservation at Nitshill Road, Thornliebank, with Coronation car. (15.6.57)

Centre right: The Forth & Clyde Canal aqueduct at Bilsland Drive, Maryhill, with a Coronation car. (19.6.57)

Bottom right: The Baillieston-Langloan reservation west of Langloan, with Coronation car. (2.6.52)

mostly been built between 1899 and 1914, but had been steadily improved over the years by rebuilding; the provision of long wheelbase trucks, air-brakes and high-speed motors occurred in 1928-30. The Standards must have been soundly constructed of high quality materials to have withstood the strain of totally enclosed top decks and high-speed running. It is interesting to consider car 812 as an example of longevity. The car had been built as an uncanopied and unvestibuled open topper in 1900, and was last overhauled in 1957. Some Standards lasted until 1961.

The 50 Kilmarnock bogies were a development of the Standards with maximum traction trucks, and were free and steady running. Although built as late as 1927-28, these cars by contrast with the Standards retained upholstered longitudinal seats in the lower deck. The last was withdrawn in 1961. Glasgow trams and track were always well maintained, and this helped to disguise the age of the cars.

The modernisation of the fleet was long overdue when the first of the Coronation cars appeared in 1937. There were eventually 151 of these cars, which introduced an entirely new standard of travel to Glasgow. There were also five modern four-wheel cars of similar appearance.

There was a remarkable post-war experiment with single deck bogie car 1089, in which all seats on one side of the saloon were removed to accommodate 38 standing passengers, leaving only 20 seats.

But for World War II, a large fleet of Coronations would have been built. As it was, Glasgow had to be content with the fact that only about 150 of its fleet of 1,200 cars were modern. Between 1948 and 1952, 101 Cunarder cars were built. They were a development of

the Coronation, with rubber sandwich wheels, and inside bearings to the axles. However trouble was experienced with the trucks, and the cars were unsteady at speed, a difficulty never entirely overcome. The Rouken Glen to Millerston route was among the first to receive the new cars. Both the Coronations and Cunarders had forward facing seats at the front of the top deck, and the cars were in all respects a luxury in tramcar design. The Cunarders were by far the largest batch of cars of one type to be built for any British tramway after World War II, the nearest approach to this being the 35 Sheffield cars.

Shortly before the Liverpool system closed, Glasgow bought 46 of the streamlined bogie cars. These were an urgently needed addition to the fleet, enabling a number of obsolete cars to be scrapped:

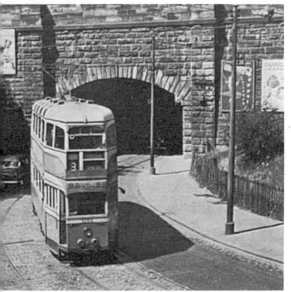

many of these had about 60 years of service behind them. The Liverpool cars were the first to be purchased from an outside undertaking; the first batch of 24, which had been built in 1937, entered service in Glasgow in 1953-54. A second batch of 22 followed soon afterwards.

The livery, which could be best appreciated on the Standard cars, was orange on the lower deck, and apple green on the upper, with large areas of cream on the modern cars, which also had cream roofs. Up to the early 1950s many older cars were still to be seen with the former route colours on the upper deck. Until 1938, when route numbers were introduced, each route was distinguished by a colour; it was so arranged that there was little overlapping between routes with the same colour. Advertisements were carried on the upper deck side panels from about 1950, though at that period newly repainted cars did not bear advertisements.

At one period the cars ran from 14 depots. Depots were situated in 1952 at Maryhill, Dennistoun, Coatbridge, Possilpark, Partick, Govan, Langside, Elderslie, Dalmarnock, Parkhead and Newlands. On March 21, 1961, 54 cars were destroyed by fire at Dalmarnock Depot; in another section of the shed 50 cars were saved by a thick dividing wall.

The track was always kept in an excellent state, and it is very creditable that so much welding was done, so that loose joints, so common on many systems, were here virtually unknown. After the closure of the line between Glenfield and Cross Stobbs in the late 1940s, the tramways were all double track. The power station at Pinkston was modernised after World War II, and was the last owned by a British tramway undertaking.

103

Above: Coronation car 1144 at Airdrie terminus. (30.7.52)

Centre right: Standard car 464, built in 1903, at Rouken Glen. (15.6.57)

Bottom right: The Kilmarnock bogie, built in 1927 and seen at Carmyle, still retains the long disused route colour on the top deck. (14.9.50)

Far right, top: Coronation car 1182. (30.7.52)

Far right, bottom: Coronation car 1144 on the Airdrie-Langloan shuttle route. (22.9.49)

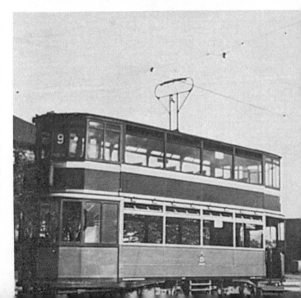

In 1949 there were 36 routes including numbered short workings. Some of the routes were lengthy: eight had a running time of 60 minutes or more, and the longest, Airdrie-Gairbraid Avenue (route 23) occupied 76 minutes. The fares were nevertheless extremely low, and at that period a maximum of 4d (1½p) was charged. During World War II, members of HM forces were allowed to travel any distance for 1d (.4p)! The running cost of the trams per car mile in 1949 was 21.8d (9p), only slightly more than that of the buses.

A rapid transit scheme drawn up by the General Manager, Mr E. R. L. Fitzpayne, in the late 1940s envisaged sections of tramway subway, and upgrading of the tramways to light railways. However in 1951 it was decided to shelve the Fitzpayne Plan, to scrap the trams, and to give up out-boundary portions of routes to the British Transport Commission bus companies.

This resulted in some routes being arbitrarily cut short, and for a time Baillieston and Maryhill were termini. The tramways more than covered their operating costs at the time the scrapping decision was reached. The overriding reason for the removal of the trams is to be seen in the proposed co-ordination with BTC road and rail services, together with an anticipated reduction in congestion in the central streets.

On May 24, 1950 occurred the worst post-war accident on a British tramway, when seven persons were killed and 43 injured in a collision between a tram and a bus in Great Western Road. A Corporation bus was going towards the City, and a Standard car to Dalmuir West, when the bus overturned in the path of the tram. The tram crashed into the roof of the bus, and embedded itself in the ceiling of the lower deck. Nearly all the casualties were in the bus.

The General Manager submitted a report in 1955, in which it was proposed that ten tram routes should be converted in the ensuing five years, eight to bus and two to trolleybus, in order to eliminate the 300 oldest cars. It will be seen that most of the tram routes, including the long out-boundary routes, were converted to bus operation.

The last day of normal tramway operation was September 1, 1962, when route 9 from Dalmuir West to Auchenshuggle, running from Dalmarnock Depot, was closed. From September 2 to 4 there was a special service from Auchenshuggle to Anderston Cross. A ceremonial procession from Dalmarnock to Coplawhill took place on September 4, the last car of all in the Clydesbank ceremony being Coronation 1282. Glasgow had been the last British industrial city with trams, which were also the last of the traditional type of tramway running mainly in the street.

Top right: Four-wheel car 1001 at Elderslie terminus. (4.6.52)

Right: Cunarder car 1333 at Rouken Glen. (Sept 1949)

Far right, top: Cunarder car 1354 at Hillingdon Road. (16.6.57)

Far right, bottom: Ex-Liverpool car at Milngavie. (14.6.54)

Dundee

Dundee was once described as the city of 'Jute, Jam and Journalism', and owes its rise to the fine situation on the Firth of Tay. Horse tramways commenced in Dundee in 1877, and from 1885 some routes were steam worked. Electric trams started running in 1900, the maximum route mileage of standard gauge track reaching 15½.

A notable feature of the High Street was the kerbside loading bay for Downfield and Maryfield cars. The system included some fair gradients, and a peculiarity of the Blackness and Ninewells routes was that they were only a few minutes' walk apart for the whole of their length.

The backbone of the fleet were the much-rebuilt older cars. The Lochee route was worked by the Lochee type built in 1930: they could be identified by the flush-panelled sides, and had very comfortable seating. The livery of the fleet was apple green and cream, enhanced by full lining-out, which by the mid-1950s was becoming rare. Up to about 1950, no advertising was carried, so that the coat of arms appeared not only on the waist panels, but also on the ends of the cars! The cars were always kept well maintained and clean, although the cost was reflected in the very high operating figure (for 1949) of 26.5d (11p) per car mile: even so they were more economic than the buses. Depots were at Maryfield and Lochee, the latter also accommodating the works.

The track was very well maintained, being some of the very best on British tramways. Three main services were worked: Maryfield — Ninewells, Lochee — High Street, and Blackness — Downfield. Lochee had a service of four minutes or less, Maryfield and Downfield 4-6 minutes, Blackness about eight minutes, and Ninewells about 12 minutes. Cars to Downfield ran alternately via Hilltown and Moncur Crescent, but from 1953 all cars ran via Hilltown, Moncur Crescent being kept intact.

There was still a 1d (.4p) minimum (child ½d) fare in 1948! The maximum fare for all other journeys was 2½d (1p), except that Maryfield — Ninewells and Blackness — Downfield cost 3d. The 2½d fare gave about three miles of travel. Transfers to the value of 2d and 2½d were issued on the Downfield route only. Parcels were carried on the cars for delivery in the City area.

A report by the General Manager in 1949 stated that 18 of the 56 cars had bodywork nearly 50 years old, and suggested the possibility of purchasing new rolling stock. It was still the intention at the end of 1951 to retain trams on the 12¼ miles of route as the main form of transport, to enlarge the fleet if necessary, and replace old cars by new ones. It was proposed that the buses should serve only as tramway feeders. However these plans came to nothing, and yet another efficient small tramway system was doomed: closure took place in the space of one year, the last car running on October 20, 1956.

HIGH STREET TO·NINEWELLS
WEEKDAYS

am	am	am	pm	pm	pm	pm	pm	pm
5.53	8.10	10.0	12.0	2.0	4.0	6.0	8.0	10.0
6.15	8.20	10.12	12.12	2.12	4.12	6.12	8.12	10.12
6.50	8.30	10.24	12.24	2.24	4.24	6.24	8.24	10.24
7.0	8.40	10.36	12.36	2.36	4.36	6.36	8.36	10.36
7.10	8.50	10.48	12.49	2.48	4.48	6.48	8.48	10.48
7.20	9.0	11.0	1.0	3.0	5.0	7.0	9.0	11.0
7.30	9.12	11.12	1.12	3.12	5.12	7.12	9.12	11.15
7.40	9.24	11.24	1.24	3.24	5.24	7.24	9.24	11.30
7.50	9.36	11.36	1.36	3.36	5.36	7.36	9.36	
8.0	9.48	11.49	1.48	3.48	5.48	7.48	9.48	

SATURDAYS—As on weekdays until 11.0 p.m. At 11.12 p.m. and 11.30 p.m.

SUNDAYS—At 8.50 a.m., 9.5, 9.23, 9.42, 10.0, 10.6, 10.12, 10.18, 10.23, 10.28, 10.36, 10.49, 10.54, and 11.0 a.m. At 11.6 a.m. and every 8 minutes until 11.46 a.m. At 11.54 a.m. and every 6 minutes until 11.0 p.m., then 11.15 p.m.

NINEWELLS TO HIGH STREET
WEEKDAYS

am	am	am	pm	pm	pm	pm	pm	pm
6.20	8.27	10.21	12.21	2.21	4.21	6.21	8.21	10.21
6.35	8.37	10.33	12.33	2.33	4.33	6.33	8.33	10.33
7.7	8.47	10.45	12.45	2.45	4.45	6.45	8.45	10.45
7.17	8.57	10.57	12.57	2.57	4.57	6.57	8.57	10.57
7.27	9.9	11.9	1.9	3.9	5.9	7.9	9.9	11.9
7.37	9.21	11.21	1.21	3.21	5.21	7.21	9.21	11.21
7.47	9.33	11.33	1.33	3.33	5.33	7.33	9.33	11.36
7.57	9.45	11.45	1.45	3.45	5.45	7.45	9.45	11.46
8.7	9.57	11.57	1.57	3.57	5.57	7.57	9.57	
8.17	10.9	12.9	2.9	4.9	6.9	8.9	10.9	

SATURDAYS—As on weekdays

SUNDAYS—At 9.5 a.m., 9.22, 9.40, 9.59, 10.17, 10.23, 10.29, 10.35, 10.39, 10.44, 10.52, 11.3, 11.10, 11.17, 11.23, 11.31, 11.39, 11.47, 11.55 a.m., 12.3 p,m, At 12.11 p.m. and every 6 minutes until 11.11 p.m., then 11.21 and 11.31 p.m.

Bottom left: High Street. (17.6.54)

Left: The 1948 timetable of the Ninewells route.

Below: Maryfield Depot, with car 32. (17.6.54)

Above: Maryfield Terrace, with car 40. (22.7.52)

Left: Car 29 at Balgay Road. (22.7.52)

Top right: A long single track section near Ninewells terminus. (17.6.54)

Bottom right: Car 30 at Lochee terminus (22.7.52)

Edinburgh

Meanwhile the Musselburgh & District Electric Light & Traction Co Ltd had opened the Joppa to Levenhall line in 1904, the electric cars being extended to Port Seton in 1909. The Leith electric system was inaugurated in 1905, and at that period Leith was still separate from Edinburgh. No through working between Edinburgh and either of the two systems, which met at Joppa and Pilrig respectively, was of course possible, because of the different methods of traction, but all lines were built to a gauge of 4ft 8½in. The first electric line in Edinburgh started working in 1910 from Ardmillan Terrace to Slateford, four cable cars being converted for the service.

Although the hilly topography of Edinburgh made it unsuitable for that form of transport, the first horse tramway opened in 1871. In 1888 the first cable route was opened between Hanover Street and Goldenacre; by 1908 there were 26 miles of route worked by 200 cars, making it the fourth largest cable system in the world, indeed a mechanical marvel of the first order. The cable ran in a conduit beneath the rails, and could be gripped or released at will. Auxiliary cables were employed on curves and at depot entrances; certain portions of track, where cars could coast, were not provided with a cable. The considerable capital investment in the cable tramways largely explains the late conversion to electric traction.

Below: View looking from Waterloo Place towards Princes Street, with the Scott Monument in the background. These tracks, with the cable conduit still in place, were not in regular use. (16.9.50)

Top right: Princes Street at Post Office, with streamlined car 18. (1.6.52)

Centre right: Car 235 climbing the Mound, near Princes Street. (1.8.54)

Bottom right: North Bridge, near Post Office. (15.9.50)

In 1919 the City took over the working of the system from the Edinburgh & District Tramways Co Ltd. The Edinburgh boundary was extended to include Leith in 1920, so that the Leith tramways came under Edinburgh's control. No time was lost in abolishing the cable tramways; their abandonment started in October 1920, some routes being temporarily replaced by buses until the electric cars could commence. Electric traction over ex-cable routes started in June 1922, the original rolling stock being converted cable cars. Although the last cable car ran on the Joppa route in 1923, when through cars were extended from Waterloo Place to Port Seton, the cable routes were not finally electrified until 1924. The late electrification of the tramways was a great advantage insofar as Edinburgh then possessed a modern system by comparison with other towns, with substantial equipment of high standard. It is ironic that Mr R. Stuart Pilcher was responsible for both the reconstruction of the Edinburgh tramways and the early start of the abandonment of the Manchester system.

The Portobello & Musselburgh company gave up working their trams in 1928, when the section beyond Levenhall was closed, but Edinburgh continued to run cars as far as Levenhall. The Joppa-Levenhall portion was acquired by Edinburgh in 1931.

There were some extensions beyond the ex-cable routes. New lines were opened in George Street (parallel to Princes Street) and in Melville Drive in 1925, and from Craiglockhart to Colinton in 1926.

Far left, top: Track relaying in Leith Walk. (5.6.52)

Far left, bottom: View looking towards Leith Street from Broughton Street. (18.6.54)

Above: Melville Drive, Marchmont Road, with cars 190 (left) and 232. (12.6.54)

Left: Car 212 at Fairmilehead terminus. (10.8.51)

The last extensions to the system were from Liberton to Liberton Dams in 1935, from Braids to Fairmilehead in 1936, and the final stage of the Corstorphine extension to Maybury terminus in 1937. The latter was the last new extension, bringing the route mileage to 47, of which just over 1½ miles were single track. In 1939 work started on an extension along Ferry Road to Crewe Road Toll, commencing from the new terminus, and parts of both tracks were laid, overhead standards erected, and the road widened; a junction was also inserted in Granton Road. However at the outbreak of World War II work ceased and never restarted, and there are few examples in Britain of so much construction being carried out but never completed!

An extremely good feature of the tramways was that almost every stop in the central area had loading islands; this was made possible by the generous street layout. The stops were moreover clearly marked with route numbers and the name of the stop. Although there was no reserved track, the line on the very wide

Above: Corstorphine terminus, with car 63. (2.8.52)

Right: Firrhill, near Colinton terminus, with car 277 in foreground. (23.7.52)

Centre right: Car 300 descending a steep curve on Howe Street, shortly after leaving Waverley terminus, on the last day of operation of the Comely Bank route. (31.5.52)

Bottom right: Comely Bank terminus, with car 308. (5.8.51)

Far right, top: Car 168 at Granton. (5.8.51)

Far right, bottom: Cars 219 (in foreground) and 50 at Stanley Road terminus. (5.8.51)

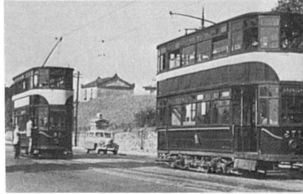

Princes Street was a kind of semi-reservation. The paralleling George Street was never used to any extent to relieve the pressure on Princes Street; an attempt by the undertaking to put more services along George Street met with little response from the public, who waited for following Princes Street cars.

A notable feature of the Edinburgh tramways were the gradients, mainly to be found on the southern routes, which climbed steadily toward their termini. In the City centre there was a steep climb up to the Mound from Princes Street.

The southern routes generally served superior living areas, and the inner suburbs were served by a network of circular routes worked by services 6, 13 and 14, the last two of which also described a circle through Leith and Granton. At Morningside Station there was a terminal stub for route 5. The Liberton, Fairmilehead

Above: Stanley Road terminus, showing the unusual centre pole construction, with car 214. (3.6.52)

Above right: Leith Docks Swing Bridge, with car 249. (15.9.50)

Centre right: Car 370 and ex-Manchester 404 (in foreground) at Waterloo Place terminus. (15.9.50)

Bottom right: Ex-Manchester car 407 in Waterloo Place, near the terminus. (3.8.51)

and Corstorphine routes ran along broad thoroughfares, but those to Colinton, Slateford and Stenhouse followed narrower roads.

The north side routes varied between route 24 from Waverley to Comely Bank (1½ miles) and route 21 from Post Office to Levenhall (7 miles). Leith and Granton were well served by circular services, and the complex track layout had not a single dead-end. At Leith Docks there was an impressive opening swing bridge.

The roads on the northern routes were generally not very wide, and at Trinity Road, Newhaven an S-bend under a railway bridge was protected by light signals. The outer portion of the Levenhall route included some single track. Between Granton and Levenhall the trams ran alongside the Firth of Forth for considerable distances. There was a particularly attractive section at Musselburgh, where the tramway crossed the River Esk. The only out-boundary part of the system was traversed between Eastfield (just east of Joppa) and Levenhall.

Many cable cars were reconstructed and mounted on four-wheel trucks, but at least one cable car had electric motors fitted to the bogies experimentally. In all about 164 cable cars were converted to electric operation, but some ran at first in open top condition.

Standard electric cars started to be delivered in 1922. On completion of the work of converting cable cars, Shrubhill Works started to build new electric cars in 1924.

A turning point was reached with the completion of car 180 at Shrubhill in 1932: the body was of composite construction, and the upper saloon had no bulkheads. Cars 260 and 265, similar to 180, but of all-metal construction, were delivered by outside builders in 1933.

Twelve modern metal-bodied cars were delivered in 1934, three having a pronounced rake at the ends, so that they were known as 'streamlined' cars. A further batch of 20 streamlined cars was also delivered from outside builders in 1935. The metal-bodied cars were commonly seen on circular routes 13/14, and streamlined cars on the Joppa and Levenhall routes.

In 1934 the first of the new Standard cars appeared from Shrubhill. A steady flow of new cars was produced until 1939, the pace slowing until production ceased with the last three bodies in 1950. The new vehicles latterly replaced the oldest of the cars built new as electrics. Altogether about 84 modern Standard cars were turned out by Shrubhill. All the cars had compatible trucks and motors; they were fitted with the same pattern of air brake, hence there was a uniform standard of performance on all services, and good average speeds were maintained.

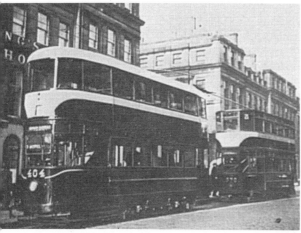

Eleven Pilcher cars built in 1930 were obtained from Manchester in 1946. Designed by a former manager of the Edinburgh tramways, these cars compared unfavourably in construction and comfort with the oldest Edinburgh trams. Originally allocated to Joppa Depot, they normally ran on the Levenhall service.

The fleet reached a maximum of 356 cars about 1950. Routes were identified at night by the use of two coloured lights immediately below the route number; however on the streamlined and ex-Manchester cars the lights were in the end upper deck panelling. In addition coloured route boards were displayed in the side windows, and where appropriate, in the driver's window. Pennants were flown from the trolley rope on special occasions! The livery was maroon and white, with gold lining, window frames being brown. Advertising was not carried until 1952, and then only on the upper deck side panel.

The maintenance of the cars deteriorated rapidly from about 1950 onwards, with evidence of body working on the older vehicles; flat wheels were frequent.

Depots were situated at Georgie, Tollcross, Shrubhill, Leith Walk and Joppa. The site of Joppa Depot was severely restricted with the result that the shed fan leading to the storage tracks inside the depot had to be incorporated into one of the running tracks. Hence it was subject to considerable wear, and the cars generated much noise in negotiating the frequent points along this length. The works and permanent way yard were at Shrubhill. Most of Princes Street was relaid about 1950-52. There was considerable relaying of track at least until 1952, but as early as

1950 it was noted that some track was badly corrugated; on the Corstorphine route in the Murrayfield area the rails were badly worn. The overhead was of span wire construction, but centre poles were to be found in Princes Street, Leith Walk and Stanley Road.

With the exception of route 24 and those terminating at Waterloo Place, all routes ran through across the City centre. In 1950-51 175 million passengers were carried by the trams, which ran 13.5 million miles.

Even with the fare increase of February 1951, the maximum tram fare was still only 3d (1p), for which it was possible to travel 6¼ miles! At this period 3d and 4d workmen's tickets were issued on the trams; free travel was available for war disabled and blind persons. Season tickets were still issued on the Waterloo Place to Joppa section only, the cost being £3 for three months.

In 1950-51 the working expenses of 20.4d (8p) per car mile were low in comparison with most other British systems. The trams always ran at a profit from 1920 at least until 1951. The best paying route in the latter year was the No 6, the Marchmont Circle, which took 26.1d (11p) per car mile. Other routes with high takings were Granton Road Station to Morningside Station (23), and Waverley to Comely Bank (24).

Edinburgh issued a very fine map of the transport services, this at the same time being a tourist map of the City. 50,000 copies of the 1950 issue were printed.

In June 1950 the General Manager, Mr W. M. Little recommended that no more tramways be built, and that mileage and cars be reduced by 25%. To this end, the withdrawal of trams on the Comely Bank, Slateford and Stenhouse routes was proposed in 1951.

As a result of a recommendation from the Civic Amenities Committee of Edinburgh Town Council,

Top left: The River Esk bridge at Musselburgh. (12.6.54)

Centre left: Waterloo Place near the terminus, with Arthur's Seat in the background. (19.6.54)

Bottom left: Car 292, built in 1923 by Leeds Forge Co, in George Street. (10.8.51)

Above: The 8ft 6in wheelbase P22 truck of car 141 built in 1924. (5.8.51)

Centre right: Car 141, built in 1924 at Shrubhill, at Comely Bank. (15.9.50)

Bottom right: Car 176, built in 1928 at Shrubhill, at Granton Square. (31.7.52)

ELECTRIC TRAMWAY ROUTES

Service No.	ROUTE	Route Colour	Service No.	ROUTE	Route Colour
1	LIBERTON AND CORSTORPHINE	RED BLUE	14	CHURCHHILL AND GRANTON CIRCLE *via* Bernard Street	YELLOW GREEN
2	GRANTON AND AND STENHOUSE *via* York Place and George Street	BLUE	15	BRAIDS AND KING'S ROAD *via* York Place and London Road	GREEN WHITE
3	NEWINGTON STN. and STENHOUSE *via* Princes Street	BLUE WHITE	16	BRAIDS AND GRANTON SQUARE *via* York Place, Leith Walk and Junction St.	GREEN
4	PIERSHILL AND SLATEFORD *via* London Road and Princes Street	WHITE BLUE	17	NEWINGTON STN. and GRANTON SQUARE *via* Bernard Street	WHITE
5	MORNINGSIDE STN. Abbeyhill and Piershill *via* Grange Road and Bridges	RED GREEN	18	LIBERTON DAMS AND WAVERLEY *via* Melville Drive and West End	YELLOW WHITE
6	MARCHMONT CIRCLE (Either Direction) Post Office, Marchmont, West End	WHITE RED	19	CRAIGENTINNY AVE. NO. AND TOLLCROSS *via* Bridges & Melville Dr.	GREEN RED
7	LIBERTON AND STANLEY ROAD *via* Junction Street	RED	20	EDINBURGH G.P.O., PORTOBELLO AND JOPPA	RED
8	GRANTON SQUARE and NEWINGTON STN. *via* Broughton Street	RED YELLOW	21	EDINBURGH G.P.O., PORTOBELLO, MUSSELBURGH AND LEVENHALL	GREEN
9	GRANTON SQUARE AND COLINTON *via* Broughton Street	YELLOW	23	GRANTON ROAD STN., TOLLCROSS, BRUNTS-FIELD & MORNINGSIDE *via* Mound	GREEN YELLOW
10	BERNARD STREET AND COLINTON	WHITE YELLOW	24	WAVERLEY STOCKBRIDGE AND COMELY BANK *via* Frederick Street	RED
11	FAIRMILEHEAD AND STANLEY ROAD *via* Pilrig Street	RED WHITE	25	CORSTORPHINE AND CRAIGENTINNY AVENUE NORTH *via* York Place and Leith Walk	BLUE YELLOW
12	CORSTORPHINE KING'S ROAD AND JOPPA *via* Leith and Seafield	YELLOW BLUE	27	GRANTON ROAD STN. AND FIRRHILL *via* Mound and Lauriston	YELLOW RED
13	CHURCHHILL AND GRANTON CIRCLE *via* Pilrig Street	WHITE GREEN		PRIVATE CARS may be engaged for Private Parties—Terms Moderate.	

TRAVEL BY CITY TRANSPORT

that the tramways should be abandoned completely within three years if possible, Mr Little in 1952 drew up estimates for the renewal of the tramways or their replacement by buses.

The first route to be abandoned was Waverley to Comely Bank, which ran for the last time on May 31, 1952. The decision to abandon the entire system was not however reached until September 1952! It could only be justified on the grounds of integration of tram routes with bus routes to new estates, since the tramways were still relatively modern and in good fettle, and financial and traffic considerations did not apply.

By the beginning of 1955, the tramway abandonment was half-completed. Two-thirds of the 180 cars still in use had been built in the period 1932-50. The last routes to run were Braids to Stanley Road (28), and Morningside Station to Granton Road Station (23), worked from the ex-cable depot at Tollcross. The last cars ran on November 16, 1956.

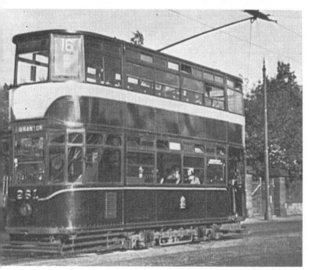

Far left: Official list of Edinburgh tram routes in 1939, showing route colours.

Top left: Car 251, built in 1932 by Pickering, at Granton Square. (12.6.54)

Centre left: Car 261, built in 1933 at Shrubhill, at Fairmilehead terminus. (6.6.52)

Below: Car 265, built in 1933 by Metropolitan Cammell, at Fairmilehead terminus. (31.7.52)

Far left, top: Car 12, built in 1935 by Hurst Nelson, at Corstorphine terminus. (3.8.51)

Top left: Car 29, built in 1935 by Metropolitan Cammell, at Fairmilehead terminus. (10.8.51)

Bottom left: Car 216, built in 1939 at Shrubhill, at Fairmilehead terminus. (18.9.49)

Top right: Car 411 (ex-Manchester 381) at Levenhall terminus. (3.8.51)

Centre right: Works car at night in Leith Street at the junction of Broughton Street. (15.6.54)

Below: Car 102 entering Tollcross Depot. (5.6.52)

TICKETS

London Tram Tickets

Single tickets issued on cars running from Streatham (Telford
Avenue) and Thornton Heath Depots in the 1947-50 period. The
reverse of the 1½d single (*bottom right*) shows the unusual
transfer to bus.